MARY MAGDALENE

MARY MAGDALENE

HER MYSTERIES AND HISTORY REVEALED

KAREN RALLS PhD

SHELTER HARBOR PRESS

NEW YORK

Text Credits

Scripture quotations taken from the Holy Bible, New International Version. Copyright © 1973, 1978, 1984 International Bible Society.
Used by permission of Hodder & Stoughton Publishers, A member of the Hachette Livre UK Group. All rights reserved. "NIV" is a registered trademark of International Bible Society. UK trademark number 1448790. The Golden Legend. Readings on the Saints by Jacobus de Voragine, Copyright, © 1993 Princeton University Press. The Artisans & Guilds of France by Francois Icher, Copyright © 1994 Éditions de La Martinière.

Picture Credits

AKG-Images, London   2 Electa/Cappella Del Bono at S. Giovanni Evangelista, Parma, 7 Sammlungen Des Stiftes Klosterneuburg, 9 Real Academia de Belles Artes de San Fernando, Madrid, 22/23 Sistine Chapel, Vatican, Rome, 24 Joseph Martin, Escorial, Madrid, 32 Joseph Martin, Musée Rolin, Autun, 46 Stefan Diller/Chapel of Mary Magdalene, San Francesco, Assisi, 54, 65 and 79 Rabatti-Dominigue, 67, 69 British Library, 70 Teifenbronn, Pforzheim, 92 Staatliche Kunstsammlungen, Kassel, 97, 102, 114 Tristian Lanfrancis, 116/117 Bibliotheque Nationale, Paris, 119 Naimattalah/Galleria Nazionale, Rome, 120 Jean Paul Dumontier, 121 Hervé Champollion, 125 Electa/San Marco, Florence, 131 Museu de Santa Cruz, Toledo, 134, 149 Electa/S. Maria, Brescia, 161 Roger Lichtenberg, 171 Hervé Champollion, 173 Imperial Palace, Pavlovsk Eric Lessing/AKG Images 15, Prado, Madrid, 17 The Louvre, Paris, 31 and 39 The Tate, London, 40/41 S. Maria del Carmina, Cappella Brancacci, 44 The Louvre, Paris, 77 Prado, Madrid
Bridgeman Art Library, London   12/13 Private Collection, 18 Private Collection/Christies, 21 Santa Lucia, Montefiori dell'Aso, 52 Lauros/Giraudon/Château de Versailles, 59 Mark Gallery, 84 Lauros/Giraudon, 85 Bibliothèque Nationale, Paris, 86 The Stapleton Collection, 87 Museo Nazionale, Rome, 90 Isabella Stewart Gardner Museum, Boston, 95 and 111 Richard and Kailas Icons, 98 Archives Charmet/Bibliothèque des Arts Decoratifs, Paris, 100 Private Collection, 101 Richard and Kailas Icons, 127 Jasna Gora Monastery, Czestochowa, 147 Giraudon/Musée des Beaux-Arts, Nantes, 155 Museo della Città Romana, Rome, 156 Alinari/Palazzo Pitti, Florence, 157 Julian Hartnoll, 162/163 Alinari/Biblioteca Reale, Turin, 167 Christies, 168 Fitzwilliam Museum, University of Cambridge, 169 Giraudon/Musée des Beaux-Arts, Rennes, 170 Musée Condé, Chantilly, 172 Index/Cathedral Museum, Girona
Cameron Collection   26, 29, 43, 56, 57t, 113, 124, 143, 150, 158
Fotolia   96 Omer Genec
GettyImages, London   27 AFP, 25 Church of Santo Stefano, 62 Murat Taner/Photographers Choice, 66 Travel Ink/Gallo Images, 71 Gordon Grahan/National Geographic, 72 Martin Gray/National Geographic, 74/75 Camille Morenc, 82/83 José Azel/Aurora, 115 Miguel Riopa/AFP, 122 Hioshi Higuchi/Photographers Choice, 136/137 Marco Di Lauro, 138 Christopher Pillitz/Reportage, 139 Marco Di Lauro, 151 Andy Crawford/Dorling Kindersley
Bridgeman Art Library/GettyImages   11 Prado, Madrid, 33, 36 Private Collection, 49 Kunsthistorische Museum, Vienna, 60, 107, 108 Tretyakov Gallery, Moscow, 145 The Louvre, Paris, 152/153 Kremlin Museums, Moscow, 154 The Louvre, Paris, 160 Koninlijk Museum voor Schone Kunst, Antwerp, 175 Museo e Gallerie Nazionale di Capodimonte, Naples 184/185 Galerie Borghese, Rome
Jupiter Corporation Images 19 National Gallery, London, 55, 88, 109, 118, 123, 128, 141, 144m, 159
Private Collections 8, 14, 16, 25, 28, 34, 35, 37, 47, 48 both, 50 Musées Royaux des Beaux Artes de Belgique, Brussels, 57b, 61, 73, 76, 78, 80, 81, 89, 91, 93, 99, 103, 104, 105, 110, 129, 130, 132, 133, 146, 164, 165

Cataloging-in-Publication Data has been applied for and may be obtained from the Library of Congress.

Shelter Harbor Press
603 W. 115th Street
Suite 163
New York, NY 10025

ISBN: 978-1-62795-003-9
Printed and bound in Thailand
10 9 8 7 6 5 4 3 2 1

Contents

Foreword

Mary Magdalene is probably one of the most fascinating yet misunderstood women in history. A saint and a woman of many changing faces, her enduring mythos through the centuries incorporates both the dark and the light sides of humanity. Increasing interest in the Virgin Mary, the Black Madonnas, and many female saints in general, together with the extraordinary worldwide phenomenon of the tremendous popularity of Mary Magdalene today has drawn much comment.

Theologians and scholars are further debating more specific scriptural points about Mary Magdalene at present, with additional groundbreaking work from leading Magdalene scholars Marvin Meyer, Bruce Chilton, Karen King, Jane Schaberg, Bart Erhrman, Katherine Ludwig Jansen, Susan Haskins, and others, inspiring many in recent times. Artists are painting many more images of her. Conservative and orthodox priests, ministers, and female scholars, too, are doing new work in their fields, with archaeologists also contributing. Academics and teachers are starting new courses and conferences around themes relating exclusively to St. Mary Magdalene. Yet, serious study of the saint has been going on for centuries, frequently against a backdrop of theological controversy.

In the Middle Ages, two of the most commonly portrayed images of Mary Magdalene tended to concentrate heavily on ideas around either her penitence or her apostleship. While these are key components of her image, they are not the only facets of this complex woman of the scriptures. Mary Magdalene has featured in many contexts, both sacred and secular.

One of these was drama. Many of the most popular medieval Easter miracle plays feature variations on the telltale theme of the sultry Mary Magdalene, pre-conversion, visiting the mercator, a perfume merchant of the medieval high street, for cosmetics to prepare her to see her lover. Others would emphasize biblical scenes of the three Marys carrying alabaster jars to the

▶ Mary Magdalene is named in the New Testament scriptures as the first person to discover the empty tomb on Easter morning.

merchant to buy their precious perfumed healing ointments as they solemnly proceeded onward to the sepulcher on Easter morning to anoint the body of Christ after the Crucifixion. And Mary Magdalene, of course, is the most prominent among them.

Like that of the Blessed Virgin Mary, the powerful and enduring legacy of Mary Magdalene has come down to us from both scriptural and historical sources, as well as many medieval legends. In biblical stories and scriptures artists found inspiration from one of the key enduring symbols associated with her today—an alabaster jar with its precious spikenard and myrrh.

We are familiar with Mary Magdalene's many different faces—a loving companion of Christ, a loyal, courageous friend, a sincere penitent, a healing saint at pilgrimage shrines, and an inspiring teacher. A non-scriptural account comes from an early work on the lives of the saints:

She (Mary) it was, I say, who washed the Lord's feet with her tears, dried them with her hair and anointed them with ointment, who in the time of grace did solemn penance, who chose the best part, who sat at the Lord's feet and listened to his word, who anointed his head, who stood beside the cross at his passion, who prepared the sweet spices with which to anoint his body, who, when the disciples left the tomb, did not go away, to whom the risen Christ first appeared, making her apostle to the apostles. Jacques de Voragine, *The Golden Legend*

▼ Many images of Mary Magdalene show her with her alabaster jar.

The biblical images of Mary Magdalene have also been connected with other women in the Bible, such as Mary of Bethany, the unnamed woman who anointed Jesus, Luke's anonymous sinner, and several others, giving rise to various myths and legends. In the nineteenth and twentieth centuries, additional myths and legends have also arisen about the saint.

Yet, like a many-faceted crystal, Mary Magdalene and her powerful legacy have also left us with other important, if less emphasized, images through the centuries. Removed from the usual penitent or "apostle of the apostles" imagery that often surrounded her in the High Middle Ages, another key aspect of the enduring "Magdalene mythos" that developed during this time was that of a spiritual mystic in her own right, a guide for prayer, meditation, or inspiration for all, a female muse or ideal for the spiritual and monastic woman, a special inspiratrice for the downtrodden, the exiled, those on the margins of society, and a protector of women everywhere—and at all levels of society—in a rigidly patriarchal world. She

▶ An instantly recognizable portrayal of Mary Magdalene, with her long flowing hair and red cloak.

permeates the whole period, providing inspiration at all levels of society, for pilgrims, certain medieval guilds, herbalists and healers, artists, military religious orders such as the Knights Templar or the Knights Hospitaler, kings and nobles, and more. And she still inspires many today, in our secular age, all over the world, just as she did in biblical times.

As is clear from the earlier Gnostic scriptures, she was also envisaged by some as the Woman Who Knew the All, as the one who may perhaps have best understood and ultimately grasped the full message of Jesus in his time, as an inspiring teacher, and as a purveyor of wisdom. Like many saints throughout the centuries, her universal unfolding wisdom and love remain as powerful for us today as they ever were, challenging us, beckoning us…a light of Wisdom and truth, "in memory of her."

1 The Historical Magdalene

SINNER, SAINT, APOSTLE TO THE APOSTLES, PENITENT, LOYAL AND LOVING COMPANION, AND ILLUMINATING TEACHER—ALL ARE ASPECTS OF MARY MAGDALENE THAT HAVE COME DOWN TO US IN THE LAST TWO THOUSAND YEARS.

Introduction

Mary Magdalene's many shifting images still inspire and intrigue us today, over two thousand years after she lived. Of all the disciples around Jesus, it now appears as if none seems to have been as close to him as Mary Magdalene. Saint, "apostle to the apostles," penitent, loyal and loving companion, illuminating teacher, mystic, dynamic speaker, compassionate leader, and more, the images and living memory of Mary Magdalene are still with us from ancient times and from the lands of the Bible.

The New Testament and other important texts refer to Mary Magdalene in different ways, illustrating her importance, power, and strength. But they also show us the conflicts and tensions that existed in the early Church with regard to her prominence and the role of women in general. In the New Testament Gospels, as well as the Gospel of Peter, Mary Magdalene emerges as a wealthy Jewish woman from the city of Magdala on the western shore of the Sea of Galilee, a town largely known for fishing and fish salting. Some scholars have also connected her name to the Aramaic word for "tower"—*migdal*. In the best-selling thirteenth-century account of the lives of the saints, *The Golden Legend*, Jacques de Voragine tells us that

Mary's cognomen "Magdalene" comes from Magdala, the name of one of her ancestral properties. She was wellborn, descended from royal stock. Her father's name was Syrus, her mother was called Eucharia. With her brother Lazarus and her sister Martha she owned Magdala, a walled town two miles from Genezareth, along with Bethany, not far from Jerusalem, and a considerable part of Jerusalem itself. They had, however, divided their holdings among themselves in such a way that Magdala belonged to Mary (whence the name Magdalene), Lazarus kept the property in Jerusalem, and Bethany was Martha's. Mary gave herself totally to the pleasures of the flesh and Lazarus was devoted to the military, while prudent Martha kept close watch over her brother's and sister's estates and took care of the needs of her armed men, her servants, and the poor. After Christ's ascension, however, they all sold their possessions and laid the proceeds at the feet of the apostles.

▼ The town of Magdala, Mary's ancestral home, after which she is believed to have been named.

▶ This nineteenth-century illustration shows Mary Magdalene having seven devils cast out of her, the act that is believed to have forged the close bond between Mary and Jesus.

The biblical Magdalene

Mary Magdalene appears in Luke 8, traveling with Jesus and two other women; Luke tells us that all three women were healed by Jesus, and that Mary had "seven devils cast out of her"—an ambiguous phrase that has never been fully clarified or understood, although it is often thought to have been a reference to some kind of healing. In *The Golden Legend* we are told that this "is the Magdalene upon whom Jesus conferred such great graces and to whom he showed so many marks of love. He cast seven devils out of her, set her totally afire with love for him, counted her among his closest familiars, was her guest, had her do the housekeeping on his travels, and kindly took her side at times."

As we learn in Matthew 27:55, Mark 15:41, and Luke 23:55, these same three women went with Jesus on his last, crucial journey to Jerusalem, and were loyal witnesses to the Crucifixion. Mary Magdalene stayed at the foot of the cross until the body of Jesus

◀ Mary Magdalene was one of the three women who went with Jesus to Jerusalem and stayed with him until his body was taken down from the cross, as depicted in this *Deposition* by Rogier van der Weyden.

► St. Peter, renowned for his animosity toward Mary Magdalene, is often portrayed as the rock upon which Jesus built his Church.

was taken down and placed in a tomb on land owned by Joseph of Arimathea. In the classic Easter portrayal, many of the scriptures tell us that Mary Magdalene and the women came to the tomb but found it empty, and in Mark and John, we are told that Mary Magdalene was the first person to witness the risen Christ and went to tell the other disciples about his Resurrection. In many of the New Testament scriptures, the group of Jesus' disciples is almost always portrayed as primarily a male group, with Mary Magdalene in a marginal role, but other scriptures—especially the Gnostic Gospels—report that male and female disciples surrounded Jesus and that Mary Magdalene played a much more prominent role.

Jesus and Mary

In the Gospel of Mary, the Gospel of Philip, the Dialogue of the Savior, and the Pistis Sophia, we witness Jesus associating with men and women equally. In the Gospel of Philip, it is made clear that Jesus loves Mary Magdalene more than any of the other disciples.

► This is just one of several depictions of the Last Supper that show what appears to be a woman on Jesus' left side. Her signature red cloak or dress assists the belief that this figure is Mary Magdalene.

Professor Marvin Meyer, one of the foremost experts on Gnosticism, the Nag Hammadi Library, and texts outside the New Testament canon, reminds us that here she is also "the companion, partner, or consort of Jesus, and the text states that Jesus kissed Mary frequently." He believes that it seems "entirely appropriate" to call Mary Magdalene a beloved disciple. Other scholars now maintain that, given her key importance in the texts, Mary Magdalene may, in fact, be the mysterious Beloved Disciple in the Gospel of John who has never been fully identified.

But did Mary ever have a physical relationship with Jesus? Some scholars believe that it is possible to draw inferences that they may have been intimate with each other, but state that the evidence from the translations remains inconclusive, as the love between Mary and Jesus in these passages could also be legitimately translated as a platonic or deep spiritual love. In other words, while it could have several interpretations, so that no single definition is the only correct one, no possibilities are definitely excluded. But in the Gnostic traditions, it is neither sex nor gender alone that defines her as a disciple, as Meyer and other Magdalene experts point out. However, in accounts of Peter's animosity or jealousy toward Mary, she is almost always specifically defined as a woman.

Peter said to Mary:
"Sister, we know that the Teacher loved you differently from other women. Tell us whatever you remember of any words he told you which we have not heard."
Gospel of Thomas

A female leader

Gender seems to be far more emphasized in such texts, whereas in the Gnostic Gospels it is the inner spiritual process and the mystical aspects of Jesus' message that seem to matter most. According to the Pistis Sophia, "When Jesus had said these things to his disciples, he told them, 'Whoever has ears to hear should hear.' Now it happened,

▼ Jesus at the house of Martha and Mary, the sisters of Lazarus. Martha is said to have waited on the guest, while Mary sat and spoke with him.

when Mary heard these words as the savior was speaking, she gazed into the air for an hour, and said 'My master, command me to speak openly.' The compassionate Jesus answered and said to Mary, "Blessed Mary, you whom I shall complete with all the mysteries on high, speak openly, for you are one whose heart is set on heaven's kingdom more than all your brothers.' "

What is most significant about Mary Magdalene in the early texts—canonical or Gnostic—is that she is a very close follower and beloved disciple of Jesus, and in her own right assumes the role of an advocate for the teachings of Jesus. She is an eloquent leader, regardless of her gender. Given the limited role of women in the first century, it is rather amazing that any mention of her is included; in the cultural context of the early centuries of the Church, it is noteworthy that she is referred to at all, let alone in a prominent role in a number of texts. Scholars believe that she must have been extraordinary indeed, otherwise such passages would certainly have been deleted over the course of time. The Gnostic *Gospel of Mary* emphasizes her sharing a mystical vision; in the Dialogue of the Savior, Mary is described as a leading disciple and as the "Woman Who Knew the All"; in the Pistis Sophia, she is depicted as the most important of all of the disciples—as "more blessed than all women"—and shares her insightful interpretations of Jesus' teachings; and in the Gnostic Manichaean Psalms

▲ Mary Magdalene gazing upward, displaying her small alabaster jar (detail from Andrea Mantegna's *The Virgin and Child with St. John the Baptist and St. Mary Magdalene*, National Gallery, London).

► *St. Peter and St. Mary*, a detail
from the Santa Lucia triptych by
Carlo Crivelli (c.1430/35–1495),
which conveys the strength of
Peter's feelings about Mary
Magdalene's role and position.

of Heracleides, Mary is viewed as the one who cast the net to gather
the lost disciples, the embodiment of Wisdom. So, in the Gospels,
canonical or otherwise, we see her early prominence; even Peter
acknowledges that Jesus loved Mary more than the other disciples.
In the Gnostic Gospels especially, we see a clear tension between
the role of the male disciples, often represented by Peter, and the
women disciples, most prominent of whom was Mary Magdalene,
who is elevated far more in these texts than in the canonical Gospels
of Matthew, Mark, Luke, and John. How each faction of the early
Church dealt with gender issues is of great interest to many biblical
scholars today. But, unquestionably, Mary Magdalene was always
viewed as the most prominent female by both, the one whom Jesus
loved the most, yet each faction dealt with it differently.

As Marvin Meyer states, it is clear that, particularly in the New
Testament Gospels, "the centrality of her role may be obscured by
the interests and authors of the gospels, who advance the cause of the
male disciples (especially the Twelve) and the place of Peter. When
in Matthew 16:18 Jesus is made to say, 'You are Peter, and on this
rock I shall build my church,' the stage is set for Peter to assume his
primary place as the first of the apostles, and for the male disciples to
take their apostolic places with Peter as the leaders of the emerging
orthodox church… . In Peter's world, past and present, it is difficult
to accept the important place of a woman, Mary, as teacher and
leader." The tensions between Peter and Mary Magdalene portrayed
in many of the Gnostic Gospels are also symbolic at the institutional
and cultural levels.

How, given her early prominence and proximity to Jesus, did Mary
Magdalene, a leader, recorded in the New Testament scriptures as
among the very first to witness the risen Christ, ever become associated with the image of a fallen or sinful woman, at best, or a prostitute, at worst? How did this situation come about?

► Peter (kneeling, right) receives
the keys of the kingdom of heaven
from Jesus, thus becoming the head
of the Church on earth.

▲ Jesus' feet are anointed with precious perfumed oil, while some of the Twelve look on disapprovingly. This "anointing woman" of the scriptures has often been considered synonymous with Mary Magdalene.

A sinful woman

In 591, Pope Gregory (540–604) stated that "She whom Luke calls the sinful woman, whom John calls Mary, we believe to be the Mary from whom seven devils were ejected according to Mark. And what did these devils signify, if not all the vices?... .It is clear, brothers, that the woman previously used the unguent to perfume her flesh in forbidden acts" (Homily XXXIII).

Since then the Western Church has held that all three anointing women in the scriptures—Mary Magdalene, Mary of Bethany, and the "sinful" woman of Luke's account—were one and the same person, Mary Magdalene. Although he did not directly accuse her of being a prostitute (*meretrix*), Gregory did refer to her as a "sinful" woman (*peccatrix*), which has had certain unfortunate and unseemly implications through the centuries, resulting in her reputation being badly maligned, unnecessarily disparaged, and greatly misunderstood. The pope was largely responsible for the classic Western image of the "penitent" Magdalene that persisted through the centuries. The Eastern Byzantine Church has never held this view, having long maintained that Mary Magdalene was a pure and virtuous woman—the "penitent" image is primarily a product of the Western Church.

Pope Gregory also connected Mary Magdalene with the woman who was brought before Jesus to be stoned for adultery, an association that a number of Church Fathers had already maintained centuries before, giving her the rather unsavory image of "adulteress." So that association, too, in the eyes of many, implied that this woman's "sin" was of a sexual nature, which has contributed in large measure to the misunderstanding that Mary was a prostitute. She has also been confused with St. Mary of Egypt, a reformed prostitute.

From the sixth century, then, the image of Mary Magdalene as a repentant, sinful woman became entrenched in the Western Church. This was reinforced

▼ Pope Gregory the Great, originator of the idea that Mary Magdalene was a sinful woman.

by the reading for her feast day, Luke 7:36–50, about the anonymous "sinful woman" who entered the house of Simon the Pharisee and, weeping, anointed Jesus' feet with special perfumed oil, and by the designation of Mary Magdalene as "sinner" in the Church calendar.

Rehabilitation

It wasn't until 1969 that the Roman Catholic Church altered official policy relating to which scriptures are read on her feast day. The Roman Missal and the calendar were reformed, and the reading from Luke was replaced with John 20:1–2 and 20:17–18, the account of the discovery of the empty tomb by Mary Magdalene. In addition, the designation "sinner" was dropped from the title of her feast day.

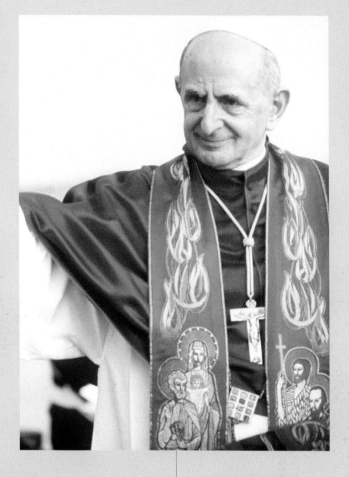

However, although this was perceived by many as a move finally to begin a theological exoneration of the "slandered reputation" of Mary Magdalene, to date no additional formal decree or papal bull has been issued to clarify this matter further and to rehabilitate the saint's reputation fully. Many within the Christian Churches now believe that such a gesture might be made at some time in the future; this would undoubtedly be viewed by women throughout the world as justice long overdue to all women as much as an important theological issue. Eminent biblical scholars today point out that it is important to note that nowhere in the New Testament is Mary Magdalene ever said to be a prostitute.

▲ Pope Paul VI initiated the rehabilitation process of the saint—during his papacy the scripture readings for her feast day were replaced and she was no longer referred to as a "sinner."

◄ Jesus with the woman taken in adultery, yet another of the personae attributed to Mary Magdalene.

Artistic portrayals

Through the centuries, many extraordinary paintings have often featured Mary Magdalene as the classic "penitent Magdalene," with her long flowing hair, alabaster jar, and healing ointments. Yet certain painters of some of the greatest works of art have occasionally taken liberties with their portrayals of her, at times resulting in some rather unusual images or details—for instance Fra Angelico's inclusion of Mary Magdalene among the other disciples in his famous *Eucharist of the Last Supper*, or Salvador Dalí's notoriously controversial *Mary Magdalene*. The many different facets of this multi-dimensional saint's imagery continue to fascinate today. But one of the most intriguing portrayals of Mary Magdalene is found in the Gospel of Mary.

▼ Fra Angelico deliberately painted Mary Magdalene on the left-hand side of Jesus in his *Eucharist of the Last Supper*.

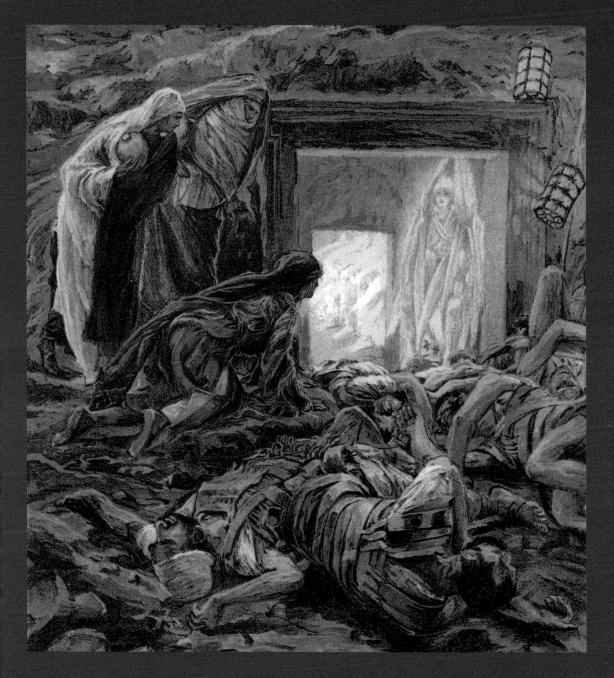

▲ Mary Magdalene and the myrrophores arrive at the empty sepulcher on Easter morning.

2 Twentieth-Century Discoveries

THE DISCOVERY OF IMPORTANT DOCUMENTS IN THE FIRST HALF OF THE TWENTIETH CENTURY HAS CAST NEW LIGHT ON THE ISSUES AND CONTROVERSY THAT HAVE BEEN ASSOCIATED WITH MARY MAGDALENE SINCE BIBLICAL TIMES.

Introduction

Why did certain early Christians believe that Mary Magdalene was an apostle in her own right, while others vehemently disagreed? While some early texts clearly stress her role as one of the witnesses, or "the" very first witness to the Resurrection, the "apostle to the Apostles", other early texts exclude or replace her altogether in their Resurrection accounts, clearly favoring Peter and other male disciples. Such portrayals illustrate the differing views and challenges surrounding Mary Magdalene's leadership in the early Church. One of these—the Gospel of Mary—is the only known gospel named for a woman, and its text provides an illuminating window into the early Church and its dilemmas concerning the power and role of women.

▶ A nineteenth-century depiction of the disciples John (left) and Peter running to the sepulcher on the morning of the Resurrection.

▼ Peter Coecke van Aeist's *Last Supper* is just one work that depicts a feminine figure on Jesus' left, a place traditionally reserved for the apostle John, the "beloved."

In many early texts, especially where the Church hierarchy and leadership system is portrayed as having a more entrenched, formal structure, Peter and other males tend to dominate; but when the Church leadership structure in a particular community is portrayed as being less formal and more fluid, the Mary Magdalene figure is far more esteemed, respected, and elevated in the texts. Eminent biblical scholars believe that this largely reflects what appear to be two opposing leadership structures in the early Church communities, each with a distinctly different view of women and their place in the Church. Every fledgling organization has its factions, and early Christianity was no exception.

The Gospel of Mary

Initially led by renowned Princeton professor Elaine Pagels, a number of authoritative textual experts today hold that for at least one faction of early Christians, Mary Magdalene was viewed not only as being very close to Jesus, his special companion, but also as a key leader in the early Church in her own right, possibly being the as-yet-unidentified "Beloved Disciple" referred to in the Fourth Gospel, the Gospel of John. While not all scholars agree that this Coptic "Mary" figure is that of Mary Magdalene, a great many leading biblical scholars support that position, given the content of the text.

▲ Elaine Pagels, one of the leading authorities on Mary Magdalene.

As Marvin Meyer succinctly states in his ground-breaking 2004 book, *The Gospels of Mary*, "Mary Magdalene is the only woman whose Gospel has survived the ages." He is referring to one of the most important documents ever found about the woman whom many scholars believe, unquestionably, to be Mary Magdalene—the Gospel of Mary. This Coptic text was first discovered in 1896 in Cairo, when German scholar Karl Reinhardt purchased an early papyrus codex, the Papyrus Berolinensis 8502, also known as the Berlin Codex. Although the particular copy of the Gospel of Mary found in the Berlin Codex dates to about the fifth century, many scholars believe that it is a copy of a Greek text from as early as the first part of the second century. The Berlin Codex contained four texts: the Gospel of Mary, the Apocryphon of John, the Sophia of Jesus Christ, and the Act of Peter. Although a copy of the Gospel of Mary was not found with the Nag Hammadi Library in 1945, it has been published together with the Nag Hammadi texts, and is considered by scholars to be part of the same early religious movement.

Such non-canonical biblical texts are called "apocryphal"—meaning they are "outside" of the traditional Christian Church canon. There were many of these, including the Nag Hammadi texts and other key Gnostic Gospels; so the Gospel of Mary discovery has been a historic one, opening the floodgates for much serious scholarly research about Mary Magdalene and her role as a thoughtful and dynamic leader in the early Church.

Several important books published in recent years by biblical scholars have helped clarify such issues about the Gospel of Mary and related texts about Mary Magdalene, following Elaine Pagel's seminal 1979 work, *The Gnostic Gospels*. In 2003, theologian Ann Graham Brock's *Mary Magdalene, the First Apostle* was published as part of the Harvard Theological Institute Series, and, since that time, other leading biblical scholars, including Marvin Meyer, Esther de Boer, Karen King, Jean-Yves Leloup, Bart Ehrman, and Jane Schaberg, have continued to analyze the texts, provide new English translations, and debate the interpretations.

▼ A fragment of the Gospel of Mary, discovered in Cairo in 1896.

The risen Jesus speaks to the disciples

What does the text of this major discovery say? The first six pages of the document are missing, so the Gospel of Mary, as it stands, opens with a post-Resurrection dialogue. The risen Jesus is answering the questions of his disciples, who have gathered in their study circle. An unidentified disciple asks Jesus about the nature of matter, whether it would be saved or utterly destroyed in the end. Jesus implies that in

▶ *Christ and St. Peter* (Van
Dyke) shows Peter being handed
the keys that would become his
symbol. Peter is depicted as an
old man, clearly overwhelmed by
the significance of the occasion.

the universal scheme of existence, all things will ultimately return to their original condition, so the material
world will eventually return to formlessness and
what is of a spiritual nature will return to God.
This has elements of Platonic philosophy to
it, as theologians have noted. Peter then asks
Jesus another question about the nature
of the world's sin, and Jesus implies that
sin is not simply about breaking rules or
transgressing laws, but is more of a situation that follows when one combines with
inappropriate things, those of the material world. He warns his disciples not to
let themselves be led astray by mixing the
spiritual with the material, as the Son of
Man is within them. He emphasizes that we
do not need to look outside ourselves, when
the Son of Man is inside us the entire time.
He tells the disciples to follow this inner spiritual Son of Man for guidance, to seek and find it,
not to be afraid, and to go out and preach the Good
News. The last major point he makes is that the disciples
should not unnecessarily create any rules other than the ones
he left for them, and should not become encumbered with unnecessary laws, as they are only of the material world. Instead, their main
emphasis should be on their spiritual nature.

Then, very suddenly, Jesus leaves them. His followers—traumatized
after the Crucifixion and its aftermath of persecution, and now in
constant fear for their lives—mourn and weep, wondering how they
could ever preach the Good News with such dangers around. After
all, if the Gentiles did not spare even Jesus himself, why would they
be spared? Almost total despair sets in. At this point, we are told,

▲ An image of St. Peter from the
Lives of the Saints. The Roman
basilica named after him can be
seen in the background, although it
was built centuries after his lifetime.

Mary Magdalene attempts to inspire and reassure the group, telling them not to lose heart. She emphasizes that they should all praise Jesus' greatness because he has made them all "into men"—meaning that he has made them fully human— through his spiritual teachings to them. Peter speaks to Mary, asking if, as Jesus loved her more than other women, she could share something with the group that Jesus had said to her alone.

Mary's dialogue with Jesus

Mary then shares a special vision of Jesus, one where he had appeared to her with a special mystical teaching. Unfortunately, four pages of the text are missing here, then, following the gap, the text resumes in the middle of Mary's revelation. She describes a complex journey of the soul, where the soul goes back into the heavenly realm, ascending to key points where it meets certain forces of darkness, special gatekeepers who try to keep the soul from ascending further, attempting to block its heavenly progress in every way possible. As the soul successfully handles these spiritual challenges and continues on its journey, it meets further adversaries until it finally transcends this earthly plane altogether and joins with the eternal realm. There are four primary dark powers that the soul must pass in order to achieve this, the last of which takes seven forms, the "seven Powers of Wrath"—Darkness, Desire, Ignorance, Zeal for Death, Domain of the Flesh, Foolish Wisdom of the Flesh, and Wisdom of the Wrathful Person. At the end, the soul is victorious and returns to the heavenly realm. Having shared her vision, Mary falls silent, and the other disciples at first seem uncertain about how to respond to this mystical vision and teaching of Jesus.

Then Peter's brother, Andrew, breaks the silence, saying that people should speak up and say what they think about this vision, but that he, for one, does not believe that Jesus would have said these things, adding that these teachings seemed to be "so different" from Jesus'

◄ *The Ecstasy of Mary Magdalene*, by Spanish Baroque painter José Antolinez, depicts the saint, supported by cherubs, being given a glimpse of the eternal realm.

thoughts. Peter defends Andrew, asking them all whether they really thought that Jesus would ever have given Mary a teaching that he had not told the rest of them about, and whether they should all now listen to her. Obviously, he was directly questioning Mary's authority to teach them about Jesus' message. Mary is understandably quite upset, and asks Peter whether he is implying that she is simply making it all up or lying about the words of the Savior. Perhaps hoping to defuse an increasingly tense situation, another disciple, Levi, then speaks

▶ Peter had the reputation of a man easily angered. Here, Jesus, surrounded by the disciples, is pointing this out to him.

up, pointing out to Peter that he is always easily angered, reminding him that he is now fighting with Mary just like the "adversaries," the negative spiritual powers that keep humans trapped in the material realm. He asks: "But if the Savior made her worthy, who are you to reject her?" Levi advises the entire group that they should all stop arguing and proceed with what Jesus had told them to do—preach the Good News—and act like the fully human beings that Jesus had taught them to be. And so they do—in the Greek version, Levi leaves on his own, and in the Coptic version, the disciples all leave together.

That concludes the story of the Gospel of Mary. It seems that at first Mary's leadership was welcomed, even by Peter and Andrew, but

once she had fully shared her vision, as scholars have commented, some of the disciples then seem to have feared that they may have only partially understood the totality of Christ's message and had trouble accepting Mary in a teaching or leadership role. Such gender struggles within early Christian communities varied; some had and encouraged women leaders and teachers, others did not. Even in later times, many Gnostic groups are known to have adopted Mary Magdalene as their leader or patron, while Peter seems to have had such a role within the more orthodox communities. But the overall scenario with which we are presented in the Gospel of Mary illustrates her prominence as an inspiring leader and visionary, as the Woman Who Knew the All.

3 Myth and History Entwined

THE PROLIFERATION OF MYTHS AND LEGENDS ABOUT THE LIFE, DEATH, AND BURIAL OF MARY MAGDALENE HAVE COMBINED WITH ESTABLISHED FACT TO CREATE A FIGURE WHO, WHILE THREE-DIMENSIONAL, IS NOT ALWAYS HISTORICALLY RELIABLE.

Introduction

One of the publishing sensations of the late twentieth century was *The Holy Blood and the Holy Grail*, the 1982 international bestseller that popularized the idea that Jesus did not die on the cross, and that not only did he survive the ordeal, he was married to Mary Magdalene and had descendants resulting from this union. Although most experts maintain that no evidence for this theory has ever been substantiated, it has taken a firm hold on the popular imagination.

▶ This depiction of the deposition from the Cross is one of many that convey the Christian belief in the death and Resurrection of Jesus.

◀ Poussin's enigmatic painting *Et in Arcadia Ego* has been sensationally linked with Mary Magdalene and the quest for the Holy Grail in recent best-sellers such as *The Holy Blood and the Holy Grail*.

The alleged marriage between Jesus and Mary Magdalene

The proponents of this theory have postulated that following the Crucifixion, Mary Magdalene and some of the relatives of Jesus, including at least one child, fled persecution and made their way to southern France, settling among the Jewish communities in the area. Centuries later, their descendants married into the French Merovingian dynasty, resulting in a secret bloodline that allegedly still exists, maintained through the centuries via various medieval groups such as the Knights Templar, the Cathars, and an enigmatic

▼ This fresco in the Mary Magdalene chapel in the Church of San Francesco, Assisi, Italy, depicts the arrival of St. Maximin at Marseilles, accompanied by Lazarus and his family.

secret society called the Priory of Sion—an organization recently proven to have been founded not in the medieval period, but as late as 1956 in France.

Yet much of what has fueled recent fascination with Mary Magdalene in Western popular culture has been in existence much longer than current novels, films, or television shows. The concept of a supposed marriage of Jesus—in spite of no documented evidence—has been a controversial subject for many Christians for centuries, and a number of oral legends and folk tales have featured in accounts about a special landing by an enigmatic family group, exiles from the Holy Land, an entourage said to have included Mary Magdalene and key members of the Holy Family, on the shores of Provence in France. Other versions of these legends suggest that while Mary Magdalene and part of the group remained in Provence, others of their number—led by Joseph of Arimathea—went to Britain from Gaul. Yet another oral tradition of this legend, which has persisted in certain circles for centuries, maintains that it was actually James, a supposed son of Jesus, who came to the west of England in early times with Joseph of Arimathea, and not the young Jesus, as the popular version of the Glastonbury legend in Britain states. By far the majority of these oral legends relate to Provence and its environs, but these were not written down until the medieval period, probably by churchmen keen to encourage as much pilgrimage and income as possible from the shrines under their control. Yet some elements of these Provençal legends were overlays on far more ancient beliefs that already existed in the area, as exemplified by the research of Dr. Arnold Lebeuf, an expert on astronomical lore and mythology. In 1995, he reported in his article "Maria Magdalena: the Morning Star," in the journal *Vistas in Astronomy*, that the Magdalene cult at Sainte Baume devel-

▲ St. Joseph of Arimathea. There is a legend that he came to England, where he preached the Gospel at Glastonbury. He is said to have dug his staff into the ground, where it was transformed into a flowering whitethorn bush.

oped from a pre-existing cult of Venus in the Provence area, perhaps another case of a Christian saint's traditions—in this case, St. Mary Magdalene—being adopted over a much earlier pagan presence in the area. Although historians, archaeologists, and theologians are careful to remind the world of the legendary status of these medieval accounts, their allure and intrigue still enthral artists and the general public, just as they did in earlier times.

Some of the monastic records from around the world occasionally make reference to the rather enigmatic *desposyni*—a group of the close blood relatives of Jesus who lived after the Crucifixion, descendants of the House of David. The phenomenon of the desposyni has long been known to theological experts and New Testament translators as referring to the relatives of Jesus in various New Testament scriptures, such as Mark 3:21 and 3:31. After the Crucifixion, the male relatives of Jesus were understandably viewed as a possible threat to certain regimes, and the members of this group were often harassed in some countries by certain rulers. Various denominations of the Christian Church have

▲ ▶ Eusebius (c. A.D. 260–341), known as "the father of Church history," was the author of some early Church records in which reference is made to the relatives of Jesus, the *desposyni*.

◀ The sixteenth-century *Landauer Altarpiece* shows King David and his ancestors, including Moses. Jesus was a direct descendant of the king, and was referred to in the scriptures as being of "the House of David."

► The persecutions of the Roman emperors Vespasian and Domitian are said to have been instrumental in the widespread scattering of the family of Jesus after the Crucifixion and Resurrection.

had differing opinions about who exactly these people were, defining them as ranging from Jesus' brothers and sisters, his cousins, or other more distant blood "relatives of the Lord." As the family spread out or fled, they ended up in far-flung areas. Early Church records by Eusebius (Historia Ecclesiae 3.20) make reference to the relatives of the family of Jesus; such early communities of Judean Christians, whether Nazarene or Ebionite, for example, were known to have had a *desposynos* male as the patriarch of their community.

As institutional Christianity developed through the centuries, the tensions between Judean Christians and Rome increased significantly, an important issue of theological history in several religions even today. It is known that after A.D. 70, for example, the Roman emperors Vespasian and Domitian ordered the family of David, these so-called desposyni, to be sought out and executed. The situation is also described in other secular and monastic texts, leading many theologians to ponder the matter further and to look for far more evidence to determine what happened to these "descendants of the House of David," and more clarity as to their precise identities. A number of biblical scholars claim that the desposyni were primarily the descendants of Mary, the mother of Jesus. In more recent times, particularly following the publication of the best-selling book and subsequent film, *The Da Vinci Code*, interest in the desposyni has increased, ranging from serious academic theological debate and biblical study to wild speculation. However, as scholars today state, no clear evidence has been found to prove the precise identities or fate of the members of this group, so these may never be known for sure until more documents are discovered. Nor is there any documentary evidence of the marriage of Jesus to Mary Magdalene, or any information about any children of such a marriage. But the numerous legends about the destinies of the desposyni certainly remain—as they do in relation to another important medieval group—the Knights Templar.

▼ In this altarpiece by Quentin Metsys, St. Anne (mother of Mary, the mother of God) reaches out for the infant Jesus, who is sitting on the Virgin's lap.

The Knights Templar and Mary Magdalene

Although meager records from medieval times have survived, experts have nonetheless been able to piece together what is known for certain from the genuine historical documents

▶ St. Bernard of Clairvaux, the Cistercian author of the Rule of the Order of the Temple, presents the Rule to the Knights Templar.

of the Order of the Templars (1119–1312), of which the powerful Cistercian abbot Bernard of Clairvaux was a key advocate. In assisting with the major revision of the Templar Rule in 1129, Bernard commended to the knights upon their reception into the Order many things, including mention of "the obedience of Bethany, the Castle of Mary and Martha." Bethany is referred to in the Bible, where it is described as the home of the siblings Mary, Martha, and Lazarus. According to John's Gospel (12:1:8), Jesus was anointed by a woman

called Mary of Bethany. A number of theologians over the years have speculated that Mary of Bethany and Mary Magdalene are one and the same, although at the same time conceding that it is not provable.

Records show that the Knights Templar venerated St. Mary Magdalene highly. Although the central medieval Templar archive is believed to have been destroyed by the Turks on Cyprus in 1571, and little is known about specific Templar ceremonies, historians do have the key translation of their medieval Rule, which carefully outlines the strict code by which every Templar was required to live his daily life.

Mary Magdalene's specific feast day, 22nd July, is clearly referred to in the Rule, so it is indisputable that this was an important date in the annual Templar calendar. However, so far, no official documentation exists to prove that Bernard of Clairvaux ever intended to mean "St. Mary Magdalene" when he referred to "Our Lady, the Blessed St. Mary" throughout the Rule, and, as others contend, almost all of the donations of land and other assets to the Templars were made specifically on behalf of the Blessed Virgin Mary (Our Lady was widely known to be the patroness of the Order), and not St. Mary Magdalene. Yet, even so, St. Mary Magdalene is specifically named in the Rule and was venerated by the Order on her feast day in all Templar houses, as per the instructions laid down in section 75 of the Rule.

▼ The Virgin and Child are venerated by a monk of the Cistercian Order, founded by St. Bernard of Clairvaux.

A precious relic

No documentation has yet been found to support the concept that the Templar Order believed that Jesus was married, and their surviving Rule does not include mention of this belief. The Rule, in section 122, outlines policy regarding various treasures and relics, clearly stating how highly they valued their most precious relic of all—a piece of the True Cross—and sets out specific instructions about how it should

▶ St. Helena, mother of the emperor
Constantine, is credited with having
discovered the True Cross, a relic of
which was venerated by the Knights
Templar. *The Miracle of St. Helena
and the True Cross* depicts a corpse
brought back to life after having
been placed on the Cross.

be guarded heavily by day and by night, with only full-ranking
Knight brothers (not squires or sergeants) being qualified to do so.
The Templars also claimed to possess a relic of the Crown of Thorns,
but there is no specific mention in the medieval Rule of any relic
of St. Mary Magdalene. Some argue that if the Templars had, in
fact, truly believed that Jesus and Mary Magdalene were married,
they would have done everything in their power to find her relics,
or venerate her far more extensively; or they would have attempted
to locate and protect any possible heirs, and they would certainly
have stated their belief in a marriage of their Lord in their own Rule.
Given that the medieval Templars apparently believed that their
most precious relic was a piece of the True Cross, the Rule, ironically,
seems to validate a belief in the Crucifixion of Christ. Yet not all of

the records of the Order of Templars have survived or been found, and other copies of the Rule might still be discovered in the future. Other theorists maintain that any alleged "marriage issue" regarding Jesus would have had to remain a private matter, as the Templars could never have risked openly holding such beliefs in direct opposition to official Church policy; and they maintain that further documentation might yet surface. After the suppression of the Templars in 1314, their rivals—the Knights Hospitaler—inherited their lands and property and later claimed to have a relic, a finger, of St. Mary Magdalene.

▲ The Knights Hospitaler, renowned as rivals of and successors to the Knights Templar.

◄ Krak des Chevaliers, located in modern Syria, is the largest Crusader castle ever built, and was the stronghold of the Order of the Knights Hospitaler.

Sophia and the sacred feminine

….I have built my house,
I have set up seven pillars…
Come, eat of my bread…
and walk in the way of insight…
Proverbs 9:1

Wisdom personified as feminine is one of the most time-hon-ored, enigmatic concepts of ancient, Old and New Testament, apocryphal, and medieval writings. Wisdom, the female within the godhead in Western spiritual tradition, has taken many forms—*Sophia* in Greek and Christian tradition, the *Shekhinah* in Judaism, and *Natura* in medieval philosophy. Embodying the sacred Feminine in her many guises, Lady Wisdom and her secrets have resonated through the centuries from the Book of Proverbs and the Song of Songs through to the writings and debates of the Church Fathers in the High Middle Ages, from the ancient female seven pillars of wis-dom to one well-known medieval topic that is still familiar to many today—the seven liberal arts. While Sophia, strictly speaking, means "Wisdom" in Greek, she is an important figure in Gnostic and apoc-ryphal texts and in the Old and New Testaments, the hypostasis, or personification, of sacred Wisdom. While "the Word" is usually con-sidered in Christianity to be masculine (*logos* is a masculine noun in Greek), Sophia is feminine. The Wisdom tradition always envisioned an extremely close connection between Sophia and Christ—the Logos—seeing them as essentially the same principle. Sophia, then, is the same concept as the Logos, the principle of consciousness, the transcendental "I" that experiences the world in and through us. As scriptures and ancient texts tell us, she was there at the very begin-

▶ This seventeenth-century Russian icon depicts Sophia, the Holy Wisdom, enthroned, in the form of a fiery angel.

▲ The imperial gallery and box in the great Cathedral of Hagia Sophia, built in Constantinople by the Christian Emperor Justinian.

ning, ever-present, in and around us at all times. This point was made quite clear in the earliest centuries of Christianity; however, the identification of the feminine Sophia with the Logos—and therefore with Christ—was later ignored, marginalized, and almost totally lost, with Wisdom becoming a rather desolate, tragically remote figure in the West.

Even today, the various branches of the Orthodox and Coptic churches keep the flame of Sophia alive in a more direct way that the Western Church has not yet fully embraced. One of the major Byzantine early medieval churches in Constantinople (Istanbul) was the stunning Hagia Sophia (Holy Wisdom) cathedral, the completion of which prompted the Byzantine emperor Justinian to declare, "Solomon, I have surpassed you!" The design and beauty of this extraordinary sixth-century edifice—the very namesake of Sophia Wisdom—also interested the powerful Abbot Suger of Saint-Denis in twelfth-century France, encouraging him to promote the building of the first Gothic cathedral. Interest in Sophia in the West today has been further fueled by interest in Gnosticism, the works of Carl Jung, the publication of the Dead Sea Scrolls, growing interest in Mary Magdalene, and greater awareness of women's issues.

There are many biblical and apocryphal Wisdom texts from the ancient world—in the Old Testament Song of Songs the figure of Wisdom is a beautiful black woman, the Shulamite, who says, "I am black and I am beautiful," in those metaphorical verses of the Song of Solomon (1:5), one of the greatest and most inspiring love poems of all time. In Proverbs 9:1, Wisdom speaks to us and asks us to dine with her and share her wisdom: "Wisdom has built her house, She has set up seven pillars... . Come, eat of my bread…and walk in the way of insight." And, in the apocryphal text of Sirach 24:33, she states, "I will again pour out teaching like prophecy, and leave it to all future generations."

The sacred feminine

The concept of a female embodying wisdom and understanding, who was later often ignored, despised, or marginalized, clearly resonates with another key figure from the Bible—Mary Magdalene. While there is increasing interest in orthodox theology circles in the subject of women in the Bible and great controversy surrounding a clear definition of the "sacred feminine," it is also interesting to note the steep rise of interest in, debate about, and study of the subject. In some groups and new religious movements around the world, Mary Magdalene is now seen as the very embodiment of the universal Sophia, as a crucial connecting link between humans and God, as an important "mediatrix" of the new millennium. Orthodox or not, much higher levels of debate about and fascination with Mary Magdalene, Sophia, the sacred feminine, and the biblical wisdom scriptures are here to stay, in memory of the Woman Who Knew the All.

▶ The Blue Mosque in Istanbul, formerly Hagia Sophia, dominates the city skyline. The minarets were added when it was converted to use as a mosque.

▼ An image of St. Mary Magdalene, dressed, unusually, in blue, from the Hagia Sophia.

4 The Western Tradition

ONE OF THE STRONGEST MARY MAGDALENE TRADITIONS IN THE WESTERN CHURCH DERIVES FROM THE STORY OF THE FIRST-CENTURY ARRIVAL IN PROVENCE OF ASSOCIATES OF JESUS, INCLUDING THE SAINT.

NE DESP
ET IS.
UOS QUI
PECCARE
SOLETIS.
EXEMPLO
Q3 MEO.
UOS REPA
RATE DE
O

Introduction

The relics of Mary Magdalene in the West are focused mainly on medieval France—here we also have another enduring legacy about the relics of Mary Magdalene, where two regions—Burgundy and Provence—have prominent roles.

Most medieval pilgrims certainly knew about the great basilica of Vézelay in Burgundy, the fourth most popular destination in Christendom, after Rome, Jerusalem, and Santiago de Compostela in Spain. That a major basilica would consistently draw so many millions of pilgrims is extraordinary in itself, but what is often ignored today is the fact that the main reason they went to Vézelay was that it was dedicated to St. Mary Magdalene, attesting to her great popularity in the Middle Ages.

▼ ▶ The magnificent basilica of Vézelay, dedicated in 1104, has always been an important place of Christian pilgrimage, with strong links to the Crusades.

Les-Saintes-Maries-de-la-Mer

A number of accounts from medieval manuscripts tell of the alleged arrival in Provence in the first century of a special entourage of refugees from the Holy Land in the aftermath of the Crucifixion. This was a very difficult time for many Christians. This particular group was said to have been hounded and persecuted, with various legends claiming that they were sent into exile, put on a "boat with no oars" or sails, and left to simply starve and die of exposure on their journey across the Mediterranean. Jacques de Voragine gives a vivid account of their journey and events surrounding their arrival:

Some fourteen years after the Lord's passion and ascension into heaven, when the Jews had long since killed Stephen and expelled the other disciples from the confines of Judea, the disciples went off into the lands of the various nations and there sowed the word of the Lord. With the apostles at the time was one of Christ's seventy-two disciples, blessed Maximin, to whose care blessed Peter had entrusted Mary Magdalene. In the dispersion Maximin, Mary Magdalene, Lazarus, her sister Martha, Martha's maid Martilla, blessed Cedonius, who was born blind and had been cured by the Lord, and many other Christians, were herded by the unbelievers into a ship without pilot or rudder and sent out to sea so that they might be drowned, but by God's will they eventually landed at Marseilles. There they found no one willing to give them shelter, so they took refuge under the portico of a shrine belonging to the people of that area. When blessed Mary Magdalene saw the people gathering at the shrine to offer sacrifice to the idols, she came forward, her manner calm and her face serene, and

▶ Mary Magdalene is carried "on the wings of angels"—the boat carrying her to Provence, on this occasion depicted with oars and sails, can be seen at the bottom left of the panel.

BEATE

▶ The *Mary Magdalene* altarpiece in Tiefenbronn bei Pforzheim, near Stuttgart, Germany, by Lucas Moser. The image on the left shows the arrival of the saint and her entourage in Provence.

with well-chosen words called them away from the cult of idols and preached Christ fervidly to them. All who heard her were in admiration at her beauty, her eloquence, and the sweetness of her message …..and no wonder, that the mouth which had pressed such pious and beautiful kisses on the Savior's feet should breathe forth the perfume of the word of God more profusely than others could.

The Golden Legend

Accounts vary as to who was on the boat as part of this mysterious entourage, but most versions include Mary Jacobe, the mother of James and sister of the Virgin Mary; Mary Salome, the mother of the apostles James the Greater and John; Mary Magdalene, Martha,

Lazarus, St. Maximin, and a woman named Sara. After they arrived on the shores of Provence near Marseilles, at Les-Saintes-Maries-de-la-Mer, they were said to have dedicated an oratory to the Virgin Mary before going their separate ways—with Martha going to Tarascon, Mary Magdalene to Sainte Baume, and Mary Salome, Mary Jacobe, and Sara remaining at the Les-Saintes-Maries-de-la-Mer site. Mary Jacobe and Mary Salome were later buried in the oratory there.

The refugees were said to have brought with them the bones of the Holy Innocents and the head of James the Lesser. Many medieval manuscripts make reference to an early Provençal arrival of Holy Land refugees; as far as claims that Mary Magdalene's relics were moved from Provence to Vézelay are concerned, this manuscript dates from the eleventh century—which is quite late in terms of the overall history.

▼ Representations of the saints being carried into the sea at Saintes-Maries-de-la-Mer during the festival of Mary Salome and Mary Jacobe.

▲ The church of Notre Dame de la Mer at Les-Saintes-Maries-de-la-Mer, built on a site sacred to a threefold Celtic water goddess. It houses statues of the three Marys and has been especially sacred to Gypsies since the fifteenth century.

The initial landing spot on the shores of Provence, Les-Saintes-Maries-de-la-Mer, was named in 1837, when the church there was officially dedicated in honor of Mary Salome and Mary Jacobe.

This very ancient site, located to the southwest of Arles, has a fascinating history. It is at the end of an area of marshes and flats called the Camargue, creating the impression of a rather out-of-the-way sanctuary. The first record of this town is from the fourth century B.C., when it is described as a seaside port, Oppidum Priscum Ra, or Ra (or Ratis) for short. An early lighthouse helped guide Egyptian merchant ships into the area; monks later arrived here from Egypt. Isis Pelagia, Artemis, and Cybele were already being worshiped here at that time, and it is believed by some scholars that the site may have also contained a sacred spring to a Celtic threefold water goddess. Historians know that Jewish migration to this area existed early on, becoming a tidal wave following the destruction of Palestine in A.D. 70, when many more refugees fled to Provence from the Holy Land. Some of these were known to be Christians.

There is believed to have been a Christian presence at the town of Les-Saintes-Maries-de-la-Mer from the first century, although the first documentary evidence of this is when the small church dedicated to Santa Maria-de-Ratis (St. Mary of the Little Isle) was constructed here in the fifth century. In the sixth century, St. Caesarius of Arles (470–542) donated this little wooded island sanctuary to an established religious order, and in the late eleventh century, the archbishop of Arles gave St. Mary of the Little Isle to the monks of Montmajour, who lived near Arles. Legends about the arrival of an entourage from Palestine, possibly including those connected with Jesus in some way, became known far and wide beyond Provence.

◀ The fifth-century church dedicated to Santa Maria-de-Ratis (St. Mary of the Little Isle) at Santes-Maries-de-la-Mer.

▶ The famous white ponies of the Camargue roam freely across the marshes of this flat landscape, which provided a welcome haven for the refugees from the Holy Land.

Mary Magdalene, Sainte Baume, and Saint Maximin

St. Catherine of Siena, mystic and doctor of the Church, who followed Mary Magdalene's practice of extreme fasting.

After landing at Les-Saintes-Maries-de-la-Mer with her fellow travelers, legend claims that Mary Magdalene then sought a more peaceful existence, retiring to a mountain cave at Sainte Baume, located in the heart of an ancient druidic forest of the Ligurians. Sainte Baume is named after the Holy Balm—the healing ointments—that Mary Magdalene brought to anoint Jesus. It was known to earlier pagans in the area as Holy Tree. Mary is said to have spent the last 33 years of her life in the cave of Sainte Baume, in penance and deep spiritual contemplation, giving rise to the "ascetic hermit" image that prevails in the medieval writings about her.

Interestingly, until 1170, the patron of this particular grotto at Sainte Baume was the Virgin Mary, not Mary Magdalene. However, Mary Magdalene's name has long been enshrined in legend as having been specially associated with this beautiful site. She was said to have been a gifted mystic whose life was surrounded by many miracles and supernatural events. Monastic women and men in the Middle Ages admired the image of the reclusive Magdalene and the accounts of her strict asceticism, using them as exemplars of the ideal ascetic life. At the grotto of Sainte Baume, Mary Magdalene, according to legend, fasted for 33 years. St. Catherine of Siena, who is known to have regarded St. Mary Magdalene as a mother, undertook extreme fasting in an effort to emulate her.

Many medieval legends at the time dealt with the "host miracles." These were said to have occurred in situations where the Holy

Mary Magdalene at the entrance to the mountain cave at Sainte Baume. In this seventeenth-century Spanish painting she is depicted with her trademark red cloak and long hair, with her alabaster jar on the step beside her.

Eucharist was miraculously brought to an individual. Taking the host was said to have rendered unnecessary the consumption of any other food. Legendary accounts of Mary Magdalene at the cave of Sainte Baume describe how she would be taken into mid-air every day at the seven canonical hours "on the wings of angels," and provided with heavenly sustenance in the form of the communion host. This legend is recounted in *The Golden Legend*, which has much to say about the unusual events that were said continuously to surround Mary Magdalene at Sainte Baume.

Even though her relics were believed to be at nearby Saint Maximin, the grotto of Sainte Baume also became a major pilgrimage destination. Religious dutifully went there to fulfil their vows, grateful freed prisoners came to pay homage to the saint whose powerful intercession they believed had freed them, and a number of medieval ladies of Marseilles were also known to have endured the steep climb at regular intervals to venerate their beloved St. Mary Magdalene.

Medieval accounts also claim that Mary Magdalene had brought a phial of the Precious Blood of Christ with her. It is now a relic at the church of Saint Maximin, although some of the relics of Mary have been returned to the Sainte Baume site in more recent times.

▼ The wild landscape around Sainte Baume, location of the grotto where Mary Magdalene is said to have spent the last 33 years of her life in prayer and fasting.

Mary Magdalene and the Marseilles area

Several Provençal legends state that Marseilles, near Les-Saintes-Maries-de-la-Mer, is where Mary Magdalene arrived by sea after the Crucifixion. Of the entire entourage, Mary Magdalene, especially, is portrayed in these legends as being the major apostle, delivering moving and eloquent sermons to the populace and helping to convert many in the area to Christianity. The most popular medieval image with the public in this area was that of St. Mary Magdalene as the major evangelist of Provence, which contrasted with the image of reclusive hermit, one that had far more appeal to dedicated monastics and religious communities.

It was said that the people of Marseilles were so impressed by the evangelism of the entourage from the Holy Land that they elected Lazarus as bishop of the city, and St. Maximin was ordained bishop of Aix. In 416 the church of St. Victor was built at Marseilles by St. John Cassian (360–430), founder of the Cassianite Order. (The saint had spent ten years in Egypt and brought a deep understanding of the spirituality of the Desert Fathers to the Western Church. He was the author of the Institutes, an account of the way of life of the monks of Egypt, and the Conferences, which tell of his discourses with some of the most distinguished Egyptian abbots. These works became major spiritual guides for many Western monks.) The monks of St. Victor and the community of the church of St. Lazarus, also in Marseilles, claimed to have important relics of Mary Magdalene—the monks of St. Victor said that their crypt was where Mary Magdalene had lived

▲ This icon of Mary Magdalene depicts the saint preaching the Gospel, an activity for which she was revered in the Marseilles region of France.

and done penance during her evangelization of the area; and the St. Lazarus community boasted that they had the pagan altar where Mary Magdalene had originally preached when she first arrived in Provence. Today, the Abbey of St. Victor commemorates its links with Mary Magdalene in the form of boat-shaped pastries, known as *navettes*, which represent the boat with no oars that is said to have brought the saint to Provence.

▼ The church of St. Victor, Marseilles, France, founded by St. John Cassian, author of two major spiritual guides for those in monastic life.

There were already a number of Mary Magdalene shrines all over France in early medieval times. Her burial place at the Abbey of St. Maximin, near Sainte Baume, was guarded by dedicated monks, who built a path and some steps to make the trek to her tomb easier for pilgrims.

At the church at Saint Maximin a strong tradition of venerating the body and relics of St. Mary Magdalene has endured for centuries. But there is an account that, in the eighth century, during the time of the Saracen invasions, the opening to the crypt was covered with earth and stones and the remains of Mary Magdalene were transferred to the greater safety of the adjacent sarcophagus of St. Sidoine. A little further north, however, the Benedictines at Vézelay decided that they, too, had the genuine relics of St. Mary Magdalene —culminating in what one churchman called a "theater of scandal."

Mary Magdalene relics and Vézelay

▶ The town of Vézelay, dominated by the magnificent basilica built in honor of St. Mary Magdalene, was once home to a more humble abbey church, dedicated to the Virgin Mary.

The magnificent basilica of Vézelay, among the finest examples of the Romanesque style in France today, is dedicated to St. Mary Magdalene. The modest abbey church of Vézelay was founded in 860 by Count Girart de Roussillon and his wife Berthe, under the patronage of the Virgin Mary. In 863, they gifted it to the Holy See. The Church always had a special relationship with Rome, which conferred on it fiscal and judicial immunity from the local landowners, bishops, and nobility.

At first, the church did not have any particular association with St. Mary Magdalene—its patrons were the Virgin Mary, Sts. Peter and Paul, and the holy martyrs Andeux and Pontian, whose relics had been translated (moved) to Vézelay in 863.

When the Saracens invaded southern France, a monk from the Vézelay community may have been sent to Saint Maximin in Provence to obtain Mary Magdalene's relics for safekeeping. This story contradicts the account of the saint's relics having been moved into the sarcophagus of St. Sidoine for safekeeping. There was no historical documentation of the claims of Vézelay, however, until Pope Leo IX issued a bull on April 27th, 1050, naming Mary Magdalene as one of the abbey's major patrons.

Matters became even clearer in the spring of 1058, when Pope Stephen IX proclaimed not only that the

This page from a book of hours depicts the marriage of Count Girart de Roussillon to his wife Berthe.

▶ The interior of the basilica at Vézelay, regarded as one of the finest examples of Romanesque architecture in France.

great basilica at Vézelay was in possession of the official relics of St. Mary Magdalene, but that the saint now had the distinct honor of being the abbey's only patron. As far back as the ninth century the Virgin Mary and several other saints had been listed; now, however, only St. Mary Magdalene would reign. To the disappointment of many pilgrims, her relics were never put on display, but were carefully stored under an altar so that the faithful could only hope to touch the stone rather than view the reliquary itself. Nevertheless, millions still flocked to Vézelay to honor their beloved St. Mary Magdalene.

The coffers of Vézelay expanded accordingly, and by 1104, the once humble abbey church was now an extraordinary Romanesque basilica. Many nobles and royal figures came to pay homage to St. Mary Magdalene at Vézelay on her feast days, and the church was honored in 1147, when Bernard of Clairvaux preached the Second Crusade from there.

Over the years disputes had arisen between the monks of Saint Maximin and the authorities at Vézelay claiming that they, and not Vézelay, possessed the true relics of Mary Magdalene. By 1265, the dispute had become so heated that Rome sent a legate to Vézelay to clarify matters. However, he was preempted by the monks of Vézelay. Prior to his scheduled visit, two other delegates from the Holy See hurried to Vézelay at the request of its abbot. On the night of October 4th–5th, during matins, the body of Mary Magdalene, which had been placed under the altar many years ago, was "rediscovered." An official report was made, describing how the witnesses present on this momentous occasion had in fact seen the rectangular bronze metal coffer containing the relics, including what was claimed to be an abundance of female hair. It was this last detail that had convinced them that these remains were indeed those of Mary Magdalene herself. Crucially, these witnesses had also seen a charter there, purporting to be that of the ninth-century king, Charles the Bald, but this was found to be a forgery. The Vézelay monks had gone to great lengths to secure the reputation of Saint Maximin as owner of the true relics.

▼ At the request of the pope, St. Bernard of Clairvaux came to Vézelay in 1147 to encourage support for the Second Crusade.

▶ The golden reliquary, housed at Vézelay, said to contain the foot of Mary Magdalene.

▼ King Louis VII and Charles II. Louis supported the claim that the saint's remains were at Vézelay, although Charles became convinced that they were held at Saint Maximin.

Charles of Anjou

In an attempt to clarify matters, King Louis VII and his nephew, Charles II of Anjou, came to Vézelay on April 24th, 1267, when the relics of St. Mary Magdalene were exhumed from under the altar. But instead of finding a full skeleton, all they found were a few bones. Even so, the king was still convinced of Vézelay's claims. However, Charles II became dedicated to the idea that the remains of Mary Magdalene were most likely to be in Provence after all. He was a devout and fervent devotee of St. Mary Magdalene for much of his life and was responsible for the instigation of a far more thorough search for her remains at Saint Maximin. In December, 1279, the marble sarcophagus in the crypt of the church of Saint Maximin was excavated. According to one account, a sweet scent identified the location of precisely where to dig. Then came the announcement that a complete female skeleton, but with only one leg—the body of St. Mary Magdalene—had been found in the crypt. It was said that a fennel or palm plant was growing on her tongue, in commemoration of her wonderfully erudite evangelizing sermons.

Charles II obtained official papal recognition for this discovery at Saint Maximin over that of Vézelay in 1295, and the official relics of Mary Magdalene are still to be seen at the church of Saint Maximin.

After this, Vézelay lost its supremacy, although it still remained an important place of pilgrimage. Today, what is said to be the skull of the saint, contained in a precious head reliquary, is the focus of celebrations at Saint Maximin on July 22nd, the feast day of St. Mary Magdalene.

Mary Magdalene, Sainte Baume, and Master Jacques: a guild connection into modern times

▼ The journeymen who worked on the magnificent Gothic cathedrals of Europe were organized according to the medieval guild system.

One of the most intriguing and unusual tales that relates to Mary Magdalene, her relics, and the Sainte Baume site, is associated with the French *devoir* guild system and the many legends surrounding the figure of Master Jacques, said to have been one of Solomon's key architects and one of the founding fathers of this guild system.

The *compagnonnage* of the French system means, literally, "journeymanship," and it refers to both the journeyman system as a whole and also to individual organizations, such as this one pertaining to Master Jacques. *Devoir* (obligation) refers to journeymanship as well as its unique rites, rituals, rules, and traditions. All journeymen are said to be the "children" of the founding fathers of their rite, whether it is that of Solomon, Master Jacques, or Master Soubise.

According to tradition, King Solomon was aided by a gifted architect named Hiram, a famous master of metalworking. Hiram oversaw the entire work site of the Temple of Solomon, enforcing strict discipline among the many men who came from far and wide to work on this massive project. But in order to assess the quality of their work properly and to pay them accordingly, as well as to expose any idlers on the site, Hiram is said to have found it necessary to establish an order of highly skilled journeymen-builders of the Temple, a hierarchal organization that was open only to those who could meet very strict entry requirements.

In medieval France, the "tour de France" was literally a journey that many such skilled journeymen would make, on foot in medieval times, to various masters' workshops to perfect their skills and pay homage to their predecessors. It was a life of extraordinary dedication and service. One of the places they would visit was Sainte Baume, to commemorate the brutal assassination of Master Jacques, an event that had taken place some 900 years before the arrival of Mary Magdalene at the same place. Master Jacques' remains are said to be located in the same place as the grotto of the Magdalene, Saint-Pilon, so that various legends about Master Jacques, Sainte Baume, and Mary Magdalene gradually became intertwined.

French guild expert François Icher's book *The Artisans and Guilds of France* gives us further details about the legend of Master Jacques and his cold-blooded murder:

▲ Fourteenth-century French journeymen at work under the watchful eye of the local lord.

After the Temple was completed, Jacques left Judea in the company of another master, Soubise, with whom he quarreled during their westward passage. Soubise disembarked at Bordeaux and Jacques at Marseilles (in fact, neither city yet existed), both accompanied by a few disciples they had trained in Jerusalem. For three years, Master Jacques traveled the country, often having to protect himself from the disciples of Soubise, who tried to kill him. He finally withdrew to Provence, settling in the hills of Sainte Baume. It is here that he was stabbed five times with a dagger, betrayed by one of his followers. Before dying, he asked his companions to take an oath of fidelity to God and Sacred Duty... . Jacques' remains were solemnly transported by the journeymen to a site near Saint Maximin, where they were interred after the usual rites.

But why would a medieval confraternity of skilled journeymen so venerate Mary Magdalene and this area? According to legend the

▼ A fourteenth-century depiction of the Virgin and Child with various saints—Mary Magdalene can be seen at the top right of the image, shown in prayer at Sainte Baume.

◄ The chapel erected in the cave at Sainte Baume where Mary Magdalene is believed to have lived as a hermit.

Sanhedrin, concerned about the spread of Christ's teachings after his death, decided to take action against the leaders of this new faith. Naturally, among the very first "targets" would have been Jesus' family and friends, including Lazarus, Mary Magdalene, Maximin, Martha, Mary Salome, and Mary Jacobe. This small group were all said to have been taken to the port of Jaffa, put on a boat with no oars, and to have made their way to the shores of Provence in southern France, where they landed. The legend says that they then largely went their separate ways, with Mary Salome and Mary Jacobe remaining where they had disembarked, a site that became known as Les-Saintes-Maries-de-la-Mer. Three others went to Tarascon, Marseilles, and Aix, while Mary Magdalene, wishing to pursue a life of solitary contemplation, preferred the peaceful quiet of the cave at Sainte Baume, where she lived for 33 years.

Mary Magdalene was elevated by the journeymen of Master Jacques to the status of patron saint, mainly because the story of her withdrawal in solitude to the very place that had previously sheltered the founding father and the master of their society made her an especially ideal symbolic figure for the guild. A strong reason for their dedication to the saint is contained in Christ's words to her when he appeared to her in the guise of a gardener. François Icher explains further:

About to verify his existence by touch, Mary Magdalene heard him say "Noli me tangere" ("Do not touch me"). These three words offer many opportunities for interpretation. They recall the famous LDP (liberté de passer, "freedom of passage"), the right of member-journeymen to travel from work site to work site with complete freedom. If anyone should try to impede their journey, they could, in effect, proclaim, "Noli me tangere," for ecclesiastical or lordly authorizations made them untouchable in their capacity as laborers helping to build a castle or a cathedral. Sacred affiliations protected journeymen from secular interference.

So the phrase "Noli me tangere" became a secret protective password for the journeymen of medieval France.

▲ Jesus appears to Mary Magdalene in the guise of a gardener. The encounter provided the basis for the saint's adoption as patron of the journeymen's guild of Master Jacques.

Icher also tells us that in tradition of the Saint Devoir de Dieu, Mary Magdalene represents, through her decision to withdraw from the world at Sainte Baume, the desire to elevate oneself from the physical to the spiritual. That a male masonic fraternity would use a female saint in this way is very interesting. In many guild organizations, the elevation in character to a more spiritual perspective is often emphasized, and here, through this act of withdrawing from the world for a more spiritual existence, Mary Magdalene was regarded as having attained true symbolic status, representing to the journeymen the highest truth of visible and material things that facilitate access to the Invisible.

Even today in France, the pilgrimage to Saint Baume features in the "tour de France" itinerary of the remaining members of the devoir, as a homage not only to God and Master Jacques, but also to St. Mary Magdalene. A special guild mark is applied to the ceremonial ribbons of all modern-day journeymen who can prove that they have made this special pilgrimage to the grotto of Mary Magdalene. After they have come to the end of the forest path, the journeymen making this pilgrimage climb a steep stairway leading to an esplanade on which three bronze crosses recall the message of the Christian pilgrimage. After reaching the heart of the grotto, the visitor can admire the superb stained-glass windows of Pierre Petit, known as Tourangeau le Disciple de la Lumière (The Disciple of Light from Touraine), a talented journeyman glazier. A final stop in front of the sarcophagus that is supposed to contain the relics of Mary Magdalene concludes the trip to Saint Baume for the journeyman, the modern-day child of Master Jacques.

▼ The Crucifixion scene at the grotto of Sainte Baume. Mary Magdalene is shown at the foot of the cross of Christ.

5 The Eastern Tradition

EASTERN TRADITIONS SURROUNDING THE LIFE OF MARY MAGDALENE AFTER THE RESURRECTION DIVERGE GREATLY FROM THOSE OF THE WESTERN CHURCH, AND ARE PREDICATED ON HER HAVING SPENT HER FINAL DAYS AT EPHESUS.

Introduction

A different tradition preceded the Middle Ages legend of Mary Magdalene's arrival in Provence. According to this, after leaving the Holy Land she traveled to Ephesus in what is now Turkey, spent the rest of her life there, and was buried there. Scholars and archaeologists believe that the legend of an Ephesus burial site for Mary Magdalene probably goes as far back as the mid- or late fifth century.

Two important early witnesses from Western Europe help to clarify this issue for us today—St. Gregory (538–594) and Willibald, bishop of Eichstatt (700–786), both important figures of their day. Gregory is of particular importance in that he was a prominent bishop of the city of Tours, located to the south of Chartres. He wrote the first definitive history of the Franks (Historia

▶ Blessed Anne Catherine Emmerich, the Augustinian nun who had a dream about the location of the house of the Virgin at Ephesus.

▼ The Library of Celsus at Ephesus, a city located in modern-day Turkey. There is a tradition that runs parallel to the Western one that Ephesus was the final home and resting place of Mary Magdalene.

Tancorum), providing details about the Merovingians, the early kings of France. As Gregory was writing at the same time as the Merovingians lived, his account tells us what people believed at the time. He was recognized in his time as one of the most careful and dependable of scribes, so, when he writes about Mary Magdalene, he is an important source.

Gregory says that Mary Magdalene was buried at Ephesus, an important city, a busy commercial center on major trade routes by land and sea, with two large market-places, baths, the famed library of Celsus, a number of temples, a stadium, and a second-century theater of Side, where gladiator and wild animal

contests were held. Ephesus, long the home of various ancient goddess traditions, especially those of Artemis, Diana, or Cybele, was also the place where St. John the Evangelist was said to have lived out his later years and where the Gnostics and St. Paul had their many clashes. The Blessed Virgin Mary was also said to have lived at Ephesus—today, visitors can see the little house, reconstructed over the first-century remains that were found in the nineteenth century, prompted by the dreams of the German mystic Anne Catherine Emmerich (d. 1824). The Virgin is said to have lived here with St. John, into whose keeping Christ had placed her at the Crucifixion. It was at Ephesus, in 431, that the Virgin Mary was first officially declared the Mother of God, the Theotokos, by the Vatican, a major event in Western Christian history.

Mary Magdalene's tomb

Ephesus was the site of two major early Church councils, in 431 and 449, a powerful place where legend and tradition have intertwined for centuries. After Gregory of Tours' account of her burial there, Mary Magdalene's tomb was included as one of the key places of pilgrimage.

It is interesting that Gregory does not make any reference to a Provençal burial legend for Mary Magdalene. In his *De gloria martyrum*, Gregory declared that "it is in this town that Mary Magdalene rests, with nothing to cover her." There is some confusion about what is meant by this, with some presuming that this might be a description of her tomb at Ephesus itself, perhaps an open oratory of some kind—the practice of burial in open tombs was not all that unusual in earlier times. So, the earliest written testimony of Mary Magdalene's fate—by a prominent churchman from France—situates her burial place at Ephesus, rather than in France.

▼ St. Gregory of Tours, whose writings indicate that Mary Magdalene was buried not in Provence, but at Ephesus.

The other major source concerning an Ephesus burial for Mary Magdalene comes from Willibald of Eichstatt, who also makes a definitive reference to an Ephesus tradition. This, too, was long before any medieval French legends referred to a Provençal burial place. A bishop of Eichstatt and possibly a relative of St. Boniface, the Anglo-Saxon Willibald was one of the key individuals involved in the consolidation of the Church in the region of Franconia. He was active during the lifetime of Charles Martel (688–741), the self-proclaimed Duke of the Franks, and lived at the very time when, according to Sigebert of Gembloux (c.1030–1112), Mary Magdalene's body was moved from the south of France to Vézelay in Burgundy.

In 721 Willibald wrote that he went on a pilgrimage to the Holy Land and made a special trip to Ephesus—specifically to visit the tomb of Mary Magdalene. But this was not merely a "token visit," as he was known to have spent a long period of time at Mary Magdalene's tomb, and he also took the time to visit the mysterious grave of the apostle John in a grand church dedicated in his honor there. He also went to the tomb of the Seven Sleepers, which was closely associated with the tomb of Mary Magdalene. Willibald clearly felt that these three sites were very important; as with Gregory, here we have another churchman from the land of the Franks firmly believing that Mary Magdalene was buried in Ephesus, with no reference to any of the French legends that became so popular later on.

▼ The tomb of St. John the Apostle at Ephesus. He was the last of the Twelve to die, although he is usually depicted as a young man, and he was the only one of them to die a natural death.

The legend of the Seven Sleepers

The legend of the Seven Sleepers describes how seven young Christian men, all natives of Ephesus, attempted to escape the persecution visited upon them by the emperor Decius, between 249 and 251. The later version of this tale, as related in *The Golden Legend*, names the seven as Maximian, Malchus, Marcian, Dionysius, John, Serapion, and Constantine. Terrified for their lives, they fled to a cave at Ephesus and eventually fell asleep, waking many years later, in the fifth century, during the reign of the Christian emperor, Theodosius II. The seven were apprehensive about their fate. Would they be sought out and murdered because they would not agree to worship the idols of Decius in his pagan temples? Malchus, in an attempt to calm the nerves of his companions, courageously agreed to go into Ephesus to buy some bread and to try to get some more information. He was shocked when he arrived at the city and saw a Christian cross over the first gate. When he saw the same cross over all the city gates, he believed he must be dreaming. Then he entered the central part of Ephesus itself. When he came to the baker's shop and laid down his money for the bread, the baker, quite intrigued by his bizarre-looking coins, asked whether he had found a hoard of treasure, as he had not seen a coin like that in many, many years. Malchus heard people in the shop talking about Jesus, and became even more confused, wondering what was going on, thinking, "Yesterday no one dared to utter the name of Christ, and today everybody confesses him! I don't think I'm in Ephesus at all, because the city looks different...."

He asked a passer-by the name of the city and, on being reassured that it was indeed Ephesus, was amazed. The baker then demanded

▲ A Roman coin minted during the reign of the emperor Decius, persecutor of the Seven Sleepers.

to know exactly where he had found his coins, but Malchus insisted that it was his own money. The man did not believe him and Malchus was hauled before the governor, who asked him questions about the treasure hoard—again, he insisted it was all his own coinage and that his parents lived in the city. When he gave their names, no one had heard of them, and they thought he was lying. When he asked about Decius, they simply thought he was being very arrogant and did not believe him. After explaining what had happened to him and his six friends, Malchus took the bishop, the governor, and the

▶ The emperor Theodosius addresses one of the two great Church councils that were convened at Ephesus.

crowd of people following them to the cave, where they saw the other six men. Then they realized that Malchus was telling the truth and that a major miracle had occurred. The seven men were blessed by all, including the emperor, Theodosius, who had hurried to the city when he heard the news.

▲ Emperor Leo VI, who brought May Magdalene's remains from Ephesus to Constantinople, and buried them in the tomb of Lazarus.

The dream of Theodosius

That night Theodosius had a dream, in which the seven men said that since they had slept in the cave until God had awakened them, they would do so again, until God should raise them once more, at the end of time. So it is said that the Seven Sleepers of Ephesus remain asleep in their cave today, awaiting God's final call. Their cave is in the same complex—the caves of the ancient Mount Pilon—as the location of the burial place of Mary Magdalene at Ephesus.

But the body of Mary Magdalene apparently did not remain at

SANCTUS
anyell hên
ARISTOBULUS
APOSTOLUS

HMARTER
ercob cyntaf
EPISCOPUSPR
prydain
BRITANNIE

The Russian Orthodox abbot, Daniel, now remembered mainly for his pilgrimage to Ephesus in the twelfth century.

Ephesus forever, as noted by Louis Duchesne in his *Les Origines du culte chrétien*. In 899, Emperor Leo VI, the Philosopher (886–912), decided to translate her remains to Constantinople. There, he buried her beside Lazarus in a lavishly decorated monastery located by the Bosphorus, not far from the imperial palace. This double translation of the remains of Mary Magdalene and Lazarus was also referred to in Byzantine holy books on May 4th, and is still celebrated in many of the Orthodox traditions in addition to her feast day, July 22nd. According to the Menologion, which records the removal of Mary Magdalene from Ephesus by Leo VI, her body was previously interred in the cave of the Seven Sleepers. Even though the body of Mary Magdalene had supposedly been removed to Constantinople in 899, pilgrims from all over the world continued to flock to her tomb in Ephesus, even as late as the twelfth century.

The Russian Orthodox abbot Daniel visited Ephesus in the early twelfth century and recounted his journey in the famous account of his journey to the lands of the East. His pilgrimage began with the tomb of St. John, and then continued on to the Cave of the Seven Sleepers, which he had heard housed not only the relics of 300 holy fathers but also those of St. Alexander, as well as the tomb of St. Mary Magdalene. Abbot Daniel was shown Mary Magdalene's head, or some kind of head reliquary, when he visited her tomb, a relic that, as some scholars wryly note, had somehow managed to "re-translate" itself from Constantinople back to Ephesus again. It is possible that although the tomb of Mary Magdalene would have been empty by then, owing to the translation of her relics to Constantinople in the very late ninth century, Abbot Daniel may have been shown a head or skull reliquary that he was told was that of St. Mary Magdalene and believed it to be genuine.

The Cave of the Seven Sleepers

Archaeologists have discovered that the site of the Cave of the Seven Sleepers was once occupied by a fourth-century cemetery that included a monumental tomb about two stories high with ten underground chambers. Soon afterward, although it is difficult to date, an extensive church was built over these subterranean chambers, with a domed sanctuary, a raised square presbytery with an apse, an altar and a barrel-vaulted burial hall. Christian symbols were found everywhere, and as many as 700 additional tombs were later added to the complex. This cave complex was a major site of pilgrimage in the early Byzantine period.

The original July 22nd feast day for Mary Magdalene also originated in Ephesus, and was first referred to in the Greek and Byzantine calendars, but was only later acknowledged in the West, in the eighth-century writings of the Venerable Bede, a Benedictine monk based in a Northumbrian monastery near the border with Scotland in the north-east of England.

▼ The Venerable Bede, the "father of English history," who is venerated in both the Roman and Eastern rites.

The Eastern Orthodox view of Mary Magdalene

The influential Eastern Orthodox Church, and its traditions and ancient history, still remain largely a mystery to many in the West today. The Orthodox Church claims apostolic succession just as the Roman Catholic Church does—meaning that each Church has always had either a Pope (Rome) or a Patriarch (Constantinople). There was a major schism in 1054, which split the two traditions and which has continued to the present day. The Byzantine Empire was one of the largest and longest-surviving empires in world history, spanning nine centuries over three continents. Its origins occurred as a result of the transformation of the Roman Empire in the sixth century, when Constantinople became the new Rome, the famed Hagia Sophia cathedral one of its best known ecclesiastical buildings.

Constantinople was also a major center of pilgrimage from both East and West, as here one could see at least eight of the major Christian relics; it was also a key stop on the eastern route to the Holy Sepulcher in Jerusalem. As Byzantium was at the very crossroads between East and West, its power was vast. Byzantine learning in all fields, and the classical tradition in Byzantine painting, were renowned, and later played an important role in the shaping of the Italian Renaissance.

However, the Eastern Orthodox Church is only one of the many different Orthodox Churches in the East. There are two major divisions—the Eastern Orthodox, which includes the Serbian and Bulgarian Orthodox, among others; and the Oriental Orthodox, which includes the Coptic, Syrian, and Armenian traditions. Although

◄ Crowds milling around the
Holy Sepulcher in Jerusalem, an
important pilgrimage destination for
Christians of all persuasions.

▲ An Eastern Orthodox icon of the women at the tomb.

▶ Ambrosius Benson's fifteenth-century painting depicts a dreamy Mary Magdalene raising the lid of her pot of myrrh.

different in some respects, almost all of the different branches are in basic agreement about St. Mary Magdalene, with her feast day on July 22nd being celebrated, as well as her translation on May 4th. The churches have always maintained that Mary Magdalene, the woman called Mary of Bethany, and the unnamed repentant sinner of Luke's Gospel were three distinctly different women, a position they still hold. As Mary Magdalene was never associated with the unnamed sinner, she was regarded neither as a prostitute nor as someone with questionable morals, as she was in the West. She is also known in the Orthodox tradition as a Holy Myrrhbearer, one who brings healing balms and ointments (see Chapter 8).

In addition, the Orthodox Church has bestowed a unique title on Mary Magdalene—"Equal-to-the-Apostles." Although it is said that the phrase does not imply exactly the same status as the biblical word for "apostle," it is nevertheless an extremely high honor and a crucial recognition of Mary Magdalene's unique importance in the origins of Christianity.

The first full description of Mary Magdalene's life and death in Ephesus comes from Modestus, the Eastern Patriarch of Jerusalem from 630 to 634. Modestus wrote: "After the death of Our Lord, the Mother of God and Mary Magdalene joined John, the well-beloved disciple, at Ephesus. It is there that the myrrhophore ended her apostolic career through her martyrdom, not wishing to the very end to be separated from John the Apostle and the Virgin." The term "myrrhophore" in this passage refers directly to Mary Magdalene—the biblical accounts have always associated the saint with the healing spice of myrrh (see Chapter 8).

Modestus also believed that Mary Magdalene was totally pure and that she had remained a virgin all her life, instructing other holy women to live a life of holy chastity. There is no hint in his account that she had ever been a prostitute or an adulteress. He also believed that she became the "chief of the women disciples"—again, this was a very different view from that of the Western Church. Before her death, according to Modestus, Mary Magdalene was said to have appeared to all as a "pure crystal," because of her "very great virginity and purity."

Byzantium was renowned for its exquisitely beautiful icons of saints. Many were images of various Eastern saints, in addition to Jesus and Mary, the Mother of God, but there were also some of St. Mary Magdalene.

Mary Magdalene and the red egg

The Eastern Orthodox tradition is the source of the now-famous Easter icon of Mary Magdalene holding a red egg. This beautiful portrayal comes from an old tradition that, after the Ascension, Mary Magdalene traveled to Rome, where she was granted an invitation to a banquet at which the emperor, Tiberius Caesar, was present. After explaining to him about Christ, his wonders, and his mission, and how inadequately Pilate had handled the situation of his trial, Mary Magdalene joyfully told Caesar that Jesus had indeed risen from the dead. To help illustrate this, she picked up an ordinary egg from the dinner table. Caesar laughed, saying that Jesus could no more rise from the dead than the egg in her hand could turn bright red. The egg immediately turned red, giving rise to the long-standing Greek Orthodox tradition of exchanging red eggs at Easter. At the end of the Easter service, red eggs are shared as everyone says "Christ is risen!" Today, in many countries, Easter eggs are colored red.

▶ A dish of decorative Easter eggs from Belarus, colored red in commemoration of Mary Magdalene's wonderful tale.

◄ A Dalmatian icon of the deposition—Mary Magdalene is depicted cradling the head of the crucified Christ.

6 Medieval Pilgrimage and Plays

PILGRIMAGE WAS AN IMPORTANT PART OF MEDIEVAL LIFE, WITH PEOPLE FROM ALL WALKS OF LIFE MAKING THE JOURNEY TO FAVORITE SHRINES. MYSTERY PLAYS WERE A MEANS OF RELAYING THE BIBLE MESSAGE TO AN ILLITERATE AUDIENCE.

Introduction

Pilgrimage was a key part of medieval life and was actively encouraged by the Church. These powerful journeys of faith took men and women thousands of miles from home for months at a time and were a popular activity for everyone at all levels of society.

During the Middle Ages, great importance was placed on the life hereafter—for medieval pilgrims, their very existence on earth was merely a temporary journey. Pilgrims saw themselves as "pious guests," here for the time being, before being called away by God to their final resting place. Even Jesus himself was portrayed as a pilgrim, for example in the famous Church of Santo Domingo de Silos on the road to Compostela. In medieval times the pilgrim was officially regarded as a *peregrinus* (or pauper) *Christi*, an exile or poor man (or woman) of Christ.

The motives of medieval pilgrims were many and varied. Some were moved by genuine piety; others, such as criminals, had pilgrimage imposed by the authorities as atonement for their sins. Those sentenced to do pilgrimage were required to take an oath before the authorities, swearing to purge themselves, and were then given a safe conduct. This listed the details of their crimes and had to be

◀ Jesus himself was portrayed as a pilgrim. Here he is accompanied by St. James.

shown to—and stamped by—the religious authorities at the various places at which the penitents were ordered to present themselves along the route, and at their final destination, where they had to report before proceeding to the shrine to make their offering and beg for pardon. Penitents also had to wear distinguishing articles while on pilgrimage, by which all could recognize them for their crimes along the way—heretics were sometimes required to wear a black garment with a white cross on the front and the back, while those who had committed a capital crime might have to wear chains around their necks, arms, or waist. But, whatever the reason for their presence on a pilgrimage, these penitents, too, were pilgrims, and they shared equally in the pilgrimage experience.

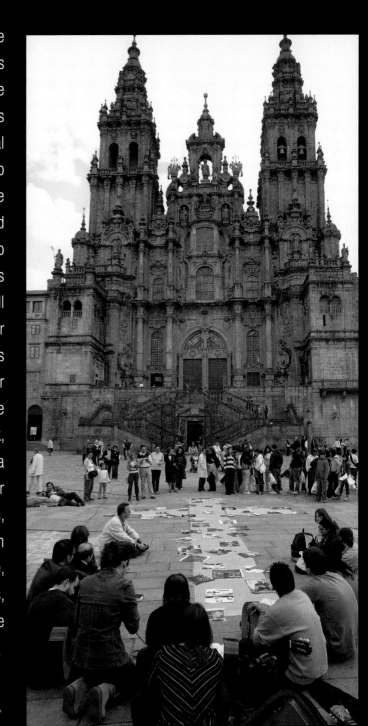

► Santiago de Compostela in north-western Spain, still a major pilgrimage center.

Gothic cathedral shrines

The Church encouraged people to make special pilgrimages to certain shrines, usually located within Gothic cathedrals and containing the remains of a saint or martyr. It was believed that if you prayed at these shrines your sins might be forgiven, and you would therefore have a better chance of going to heaven. The closer you could get to the saint's relics, the better. Others went to shrines known for their miraculous cures, desperately hoping that they, too, would be blessed with a return to health. Pilgrims included those from all walks of life—from royalty to peasants.

▼ The reliquary of St. Ursula, a beautifully painted golden box, which depicts a number of scenes from the saint's life.

◀ Pilgrims frequently set out in small groups to their chosen destination. Here, they are making their way to the Holy Land.

The wooden, silver, or gold-encrusted reliquaries that contained the relics at shrines were also very important, as they were believed to hold the power of the saint's relics, and to prevent it from dissipating. Those that have survived are now amongst the Western world's greatest objects of medieval art and many are on display in the treasuries of Gothic cathedral. Exquisitely designed and adorned with jewels and precious stones, these special boxes or caskets were brought into battle on important occasions, and were carried through towns during religious pageants or processions. Although it was understood that the saint or martyr associated with a shrine was no longer living in the physical sense, such sites were believed to be permeated with the spiritual energy of that person. For security reasons, many churches and Gothic cathedrals had at least one person at a saint's shrine who was its official guardian; at Canterbury, Westminster Abbey, Ely, and Chartres these special guardians were called *feretrars*, and some of them had their own assistants, owing to the large numbers of pilgrims attending.

◄ *Pilgrims at the Tomb of Saint Sebastian* by Josse Lieferinxe, also known as "The Master of Saint Sebastian," depicts pilgrims praying at the resting place of St. Sebastian, a popular destination for those seeking protection from plague.

▶ The stunning display of stained-glass windows in the church of Saint-Denis, outside Paris.

Stained-glass windows

People also came to Gothic cathedrals to see the stained-glass windows. The practice of using stained glass in churches began in the twelfth century when Abbot Suger, in his description of the ideal church, said that he wanted to fill his abbey church of Saint-Denis, near Paris, with "the most radiant windows." When you look up at the stained-glass windows in a Gothic cathedral today, you may feel "pulled upward," almost to Heaven itself, in the unique atmosphere created by the combination of the high nave and the stained-glass windows.

▼ Abbot Suger, whose enthusiasm for stained glass led to its widespread use in the great churches of the West.

Religious figures from biblical stories were naturally the major focus of the subject matter of early stained-glass windows and cathedral paintings. Some of the most stunning medieval cathedral stained glass is at Chartres, where, above the Royal Portal sculpture, there are three lancet windows dating from about 1150, among the oldest and most brilliant to have survived from medieval times. Both in design and in meaning, they form a triptych, proclaiming that the prophecies have been fulfilled, that Christ came from the House of David as foretold, that he was sacrificed, but rose from the dead. The Tree of Jesse theme probably first took form in stained glass around 1144, in a window at the royal abbey of Saint-Denis, and it also features at Chartres. Other major themes of the windows there include the Incarnation, the Passion, the Resurrection, the Redemption, the Blue Virgin, Joseph, Noah, St. John the Divine, the parable of the Prodigal Son, the Good Samaritan, Adam and Eve, and, interestingly, the signs of the zodiac.

The Mary Magdalene window at Chartres

Many will acknowledge that the large Mary Magdalene window at Chartres is truly extraordinary. It has some 22 sections, with various intricately detailed scenes portraying many of the classic biblical scenes and stories about the saint—her meeting with Jesus at the house of Simon the Pharisee, her presence at the miracle of the raising of Lazarus, her astonishment at seeing the empty tomb at the sepulcher on Easter morning, how she was the first person to whom Jesus appeared, and how, upon finally recognizing him, she was warned by Jesus not to touch him, as he had not yet ascended to the Father; he told her to go instead and inform the disciples of what she had seen. Because of the especially fierce devotion to Mary Magdalene in the Middle Ages, there were many legends about her. Many of these had of course already been popularized in *The Golden Legend* and would have been familiar to visiting pilgrims. The Mary Magdalene window at Chartres also shows scenes from those legends, illustrating the persistently popular tales of how Mary Magdalene, her brother Lazarus, sister Martha, St. Maximin, and others, were put out to sea by infidels, eventually landing in Provence. Interestingly, the Magdalene window section at Chartres—unlike the legend—depicts a boat with sails and a pilot with an oar; the future bishop of Aix-en-Provence is shown with miter and crozier, speaking to an assembled group. Another scene in this window shows the death of Mary Magdalene in the cave at Sainte Baume, near Marseilles. Here, we see a cleric holding a cross near her head, while Bishop Maximin reads out prayers for the dead from a book. Yet another scene shows these people present as she is lowered into a sepulcher, and the final scene portrays her being welcomed into Heaven, with one angel presenting her soul upon a white cloth to Jesus, while others conduct incensing rituals, and a final angel holds the crown of life.

◀ A transept window at Chartres, renowned worldwide for its exceptional stained-glass windows.

▼ This detail from the Mary Magdalene window at Chartres shows the saint standing to the left of the crucified Christ.

Mary Magdalene and the medieval guild Easter plays

Mary Magdalene featured in the medieval liturgical Easter play, the *Quem quaeritis*, which was so popular in the Middle Ages and early Renaissance periods that it became the model for two other similar plays performed by guilds. These were called tropes, and were pageants about Christmas and the Ascension.

► Mystery plays were frequently staged during the Middle Ages, a useful vehicle for conveying the message of the Bible stories to an illiterate populace.

Based quite closely on the Gospels, the *Quem quaeritis* illustrates the story of the three Marys and the angel at the tomb of Christ, as told by Matthew (28:1–7) and Mark (16: 1–7).

Not all medieval plays followed the scriptural accounts exactly, however; some of them were based on other philosophical, religious, or historical texts or were even taken from apocryphal works. Falling somewhere between a miracle play and a morality play is another important medieval drama featuring Mary Magdalene, referred to in the medieval English Digby Manuscript, held at the Bodleian Library in Oxford. Scholars believe this manuscript to be an early sixteenth-century textual copy of various fifteenth-century miracle plays, one of which is an important drama cycle that specifically features Mary Magdalene. Here, a tale from the east or west midlands of England tells the story of Mary Magdalene, not following the scriptures, as we might expect, but the version related in *The Golden Legend*.

▲ The three Marys and the angel at the empty tomb. A medallion containing an image of the risen Christ is superimposed over the astounded women.

7 The Black Madonnas

MARY MAGDALENE BECAME INEXTRICABLY LINKED TO THE BLACK MADONNAS, OWING LARGELY TO THE PROXIMITY OF MANY OF HER SHRINES TO THOSE OF THE HEALING BLACK VIRGINS THAT PROLIFERATED IN WESTERN EUROPE ESPECIALLY.

Introduction

Many people, religious or not, will have heard about or perhaps even visited a shrine to the Virgin Mary. But throughout the centuries many have wondered why some images of the Virgin and Child have been black or dark in color. There are, in fact, over 200 Black Madonnas in Western Europe alone, many of them adjacent to shrines of St. Mary Magdalene, and many are reputed to possess especially miraculous healing powers.

Religious historians, theologians, and art historians have all attempted to learn more about these images from historical documents, archives, and libraries. Admittedly, much work still needs to be done in order to fully catalogue and understand the history of these beautiful statues, but many agree that in the twelfth and thirteenth centuries, the shrines of the Black Madonnas were unquestionably among the most widely venerated in all of Western Europe. Visiting pilgrims have consistently claimed that these statues of Our Lady have especially effective miracle-working powers; many unusual healings and events

◀ A pictorial account of the Crusades. In the final image (bottom, right) knights bearing relics return home.

▶ The Black Madonna of Montserrat, typical of the black madonna statues brought back from the Holy Land by returning Crusaders.

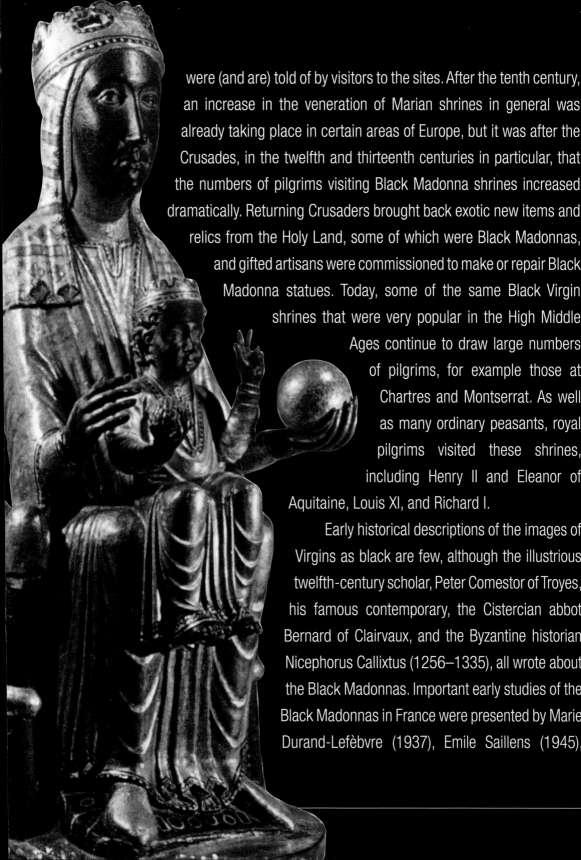

were (and are) told of by visitors to the sites. After the tenth century, an increase in the veneration of Marian shrines in general was already taking place in certain areas of Europe, but it was after the Crusades, in the twelfth and thirteenth centuries in particular, that the numbers of pilgrims visiting Black Madonna shrines increased dramatically. Returning Crusaders brought back exotic new items and relics from the Holy Land, some of which were Black Madonnas, and gifted artisans were commissioned to make or repair Black Madonna statues. Today, some of the same Black Virgin shrines that were very popular in the High Middle Ages continue to draw large numbers of pilgrims, for example those at Chartres and Montserrat. As well as many ordinary peasants, royal pilgrims visited these shrines, including Henry II and Eleanor of Aquitaine, Louis XI, and Richard I.

Early historical descriptions of the images of Virgins as black are few, although the illustrious twelfth-century scholar, Peter Comestor of Troyes, his famous contemporary, the Cistercian abbot Bernard of Clairvaux, and the Byzantine historian Nicephorus Callixtus (1256–1335), all wrote about the Black Madonnas. Important early studies of the Black Madonnas in France were presented by Marie Durand-Lefèbvre (1937), Emile Saillens (1945), and Jacques Huynen (1972). Michael P. Duricy of The Marian Library at the International Marian Research Institute, Dayton, Ohio, has pointed out that the first notable study of the origin and meaning of the Black Madonnas in English was presented by Leonard Moss at a meeting of the American Association for the Advancement of Science (AAAS) on December 28th, 1952. Moss had studied almost a hundred examples of Black Madonnas from around the world and had attempted to categorize and analyze them, making an important initial contribution to serious scholarship. At this meeting, he presented a paper and announced his results. However, what started out as a rather prosaic academic event

ended quite differently, as, at the time—back in the early 1950s—the entire subject of Black Madonnas was quite controversial for many priests and nuns. Jungian analyst Ean Begg, in his classic work on the Black Madonnas, says that at this particular 1952 meeting of the AAAS, as Leonard Moss started to deliver his paper about the Black Madonnas, "every priest and nun in the audience walked out." Perhaps, like Mary Magdalene herself, the Black Madonnas have inevitably been the focus of controversy through the centuries.

Many Black Madonna statues still exist today, a number of them having survived many centuries of war. Some are in basilicas, while others remain in smaller chapels, museums, and libraries, or are in the hands of private collectors. There is great variety, however, and it is impossible to generalize about them in any real sense, as each one has its own history and individuality. Some are standing images with a mother holding a child, while others portray her sitting with her child in her lap. Some show her with gold decoration, wearing a jeweled crown, and others are far more simple, with no ornate decoration at all. Most Black Madonna images take the form of painted wooden statues, but others are murals or paintings, and some are statues carved from ebony or jet. The thirteenth-century Black Virgin of Hal in Belgium is dressed in eighteenth-century lace and blue velvet, with an ornate crown.

In Western Europe there are Black Madonna shrines at Chartres, Le Puy, and Rocamadour in France, Einsiedeln in Switzerland, Oropa in Italy, Zaragoza and Montserrat in Spain, among others. There are also Black Madonna shrines outside Europe, such as those in Ecuador, Tenerife, Russia, and Mexico.

◀ Cistercian abbot Bernard of Clairvaux, shown here carrying a bishop's miter and crozier.

▶ The elaborately clothed and jewel-bedecked Spanish Madonna of the Sanctuary,

Black Madonnas at Chartres

Chartres cathedral has always been recognized as a power-ful and sacred place. The first Christian bishops of Chartres were St. Adventinus, who lived in the mid-fourth century, and a St. Martin, followed by Solemnis, who was said to have instructed Clovis I in the Christian faith in the late fifth century. The first Christian relic given to Chartres, by Charlemagne's grandson, Charles the Bald, in 876, was the priceless veil in which the Virgin Mary was said to have given birth to Christ.

▼ A page from the Bible of Charles the Bald, showing scenes from the life of St. Jerome.

This relic bestowed unique prestige on a pilgrimage already quite well established by 600. Today, among many other things, Chartres is especially known for its tribute to Mary, Queen of Heaven—an old tradition whose roots go back to much earlier times. There are currently two Black Madonna statues at Chartres—the officially recognized Notre Dame du Pilier (Our Lady of the Pillar) in the nave, and another in the crypt, Notre Dame Sous Terre (Our Lady Under the Earth).

Pilgrims had been coming to Chartres for a very long time before the cathedral itself was established in 1194. The veneration of an earlier, dark female image is known to have taken place at Chartres for many centu-ries prior to Christianity, according to druidic tradition. Both Pliny and Caesar make reference to Chartres as a key place of druidic sacred assembly; one of the earliest Black Virgin venerations at Chartres occurred in the grotto near the well, the location of the underground

▲ Notre Dame du Pilier, one of two Black Madonnas housed at the cathedral of Chartres.

crypt area today. Princeton scholar Irene Forsyth relates how this earlier statue in the crypt was originally known as Virgo Paritura (the Virgin about to give Birth), even though she was depicted holding a child in her arms. This statue was placed in a shrine in the grotto under the medieval cathedral at Chartres. It had its own well and special altar; the well was called Puits des Saints Forts (Well of the Strong Saints) and was the very origins of Chartres. The statue itself was burned in 1793, during the French Revolution. Many believe this earlier Black Virgin tradition at Chartres may be one basis for the continuing fervent devotion to Mary on this site today—it has always been a place where the divine Feminine has been honored. The only major description of this very ancient statue of Our Lady in the crypt comes from the celebrated art historian Pintard in 1681, who refers to her as being "of shining black colour," sitting on a chair with the Christ Child on her knees. The child is giving the sign of blessing with his right hand and holding an orb in his left.

▼ Pope Sylvester II, formerly a master at Chartres cathedral school, was instrumental in instituting a Marian liturgy.

Chartres was also famous in medieval times for its cathedral school. Fulbert, a brilliant scholar, came to Chartres from the Reims Cathedral School, where his master had been Gerbert d'Aurillac, the future Pope Sylvester II. From about 990 until his death in 1028, Fulbert established the Chartres cathedral school, which was renowned as one of the foremost scholastic institutions in medieval Europe for the next two centuries, until the founding of the University of Paris caused this and other similar schools to decline. Through his friendship with Pope Sylvester II, Fulbert called upon the Western Church to establish a Marian liturgy. In the following century, his writings influenced St. Bernard of Clairvaux, who would play a key role in the founding of the Cistercian order and also the Order of the Temple, the Knights Templar—both of which, like the great Gothic cathedrals, were dedicated to Our Lady.

Les-Saintes-Maries-de-la-Mer — the Black Madonna, Mary Magdalene, and St. Sara

One of the most famous Black Madonna pilgrimage sites today is Les-Saintes-Maries-de-la-Mer, in the Provence region of France, where there is a time-honored special cult of the black St. Sara, the patron saint of the Gypsies. Although there is no Black Virgin statue at Les-Saintes-Maries-de-la-Mer, there is a statue of black Sara the Egyptian, believed by some to have given birth to the entire cult of the Black Madonnas in the region. This whole area—Provence—has long had special connections to Mary Magdalene.

A number of dynamic Christian and native folk festivals are still celebrated here. The major one occurs on May 24th–25th each year, at Les-Saintes-Maries-de-la-Mer, where a colorful annual festival honoring St. Mary Magdalene and St. Sara, patron of the Gypsies, takes place. There was a very long tradition of several "Marys" being venerated here, and several legends have grown up around this tradition. Each May, many Christian pilgrims begin their annual pilgrimage to this event by visiting various Gothic cathedrals with shrines to St. Mary Magdalene, then journeying on to Les-Saintes-Maries-de-la-Mer for the festival. Romany Gypsies come from many places, all converging here on May 24th. According to historians and the Roma themselves, there were, in fact, two long-standing traditions celebrated here—one, the veneration of the black St. Sara of the Catholic Church, and the other, the more ancient veneration of the black Sara of the Gypsies. One tradition says that Sara was the loyal

▶ A statue of St. Sara of the Gypsies being carried toward the sea at Les-Saintes-Maries-de-la-Mer during the festival held each year to honor both St. Sara and St. Mary Magdalene.

black servant girl who came with the three Marys (Mary Salome, Mary Jacobe, and Mary Magdalene) and landed at Les-Saintes-Maries-de-la-Mer with them; this legend and its specific mention of Les-Saintes-Maries-de-la-Mer dates from around the time of King René of Anjou in the fifteenth century, although there were earlier stories about a landing in Provence.

The French historian Clébert, who lived in Provence for much of his life, says in his classic work on the Gypsies that this Sara had neither the right to canonization nor the right to have her remains in the crypt, and says that she was in fact banned from the Church. In his view, Sara of the Gypsies must have been a Gypsy already living with her tribe on the banks of the Rhône, and that it was she who greeted the three Marys when they landed. She was also known as Sara the

▼ A procession honoring St. Mary Magdalene during the annual festival at Les-Saintes-Maries-de-la-Mer.

Kali, as she was black. So, the Gypsies themselves may well have long believed that black Sara was in fact a local tribal chief, who greeted the three Marys when they arrived on the shores of Provence—not that she was merely their servant girl from faraway Egypt, as is often assumed to be the case. This is reinforced by Belgian Gypsy tradition, according to which one of their own people, Sara the Kali, was said to have been of noble birth and was chief of her tribe on the banks of the Rhône.

The Roma Gypsies at that time practiced a polytheistic religion, and once a year they took the statue of Ishtari on their shoulders and went into the sea to receive its blessings. It is said that Sara the Kali had been the recipient of visions in which she was told that the saints who had been present at the death of Jesus would come and that she should assist them when they arrived. The story goes that she did help them, and the saints blessed her and preached the Gospel among the local people of Provence and to the Roma.

Clébert says that until 1912, only Gypsies had the right to go inside the church crypt during this May celebration. They spent a whole night there, holding a vigil. Experts have examined the statue of St. Sara there several times, and believe that it must have replaced a far more ancient wooden statue, as the current one dates from as late as the eighteenth century.

In the twenty-first century, many groups from many different places—Christians, Gypsies, and the general public—still come together to celebrate in this place, which has such strong associations with St. Mary Magdalene. The memory of black St. Sara—whoever she was—will clearly live on for some time to come.

▲ Black St. Sara is venerated during the annual all-night vigil in the crypt of the church at Les-Saintes-Maries-de-la-Mer.

8 The Alabaster Jar –an Enduring Symbol

MARY MAGDALENE'S TRADEMARK SYMBOL IS HER ALABASTER JAR, AND MOST PORTRAYALS OF THE SAINT INCLUDE THIS ARTIFACT. BUT WHAT IS THE IMPORTANCE OF THIS JAR IN THE STORY OF MARY MAGDALENE?

Introduction

....And when the sabbath was past, Mary Magdalene, and Mary the mother of James, and Salome, bought spices, so that they might go and anoint him. Mark 16:1

The alabaster jar, perfumes, and ointments have long been associated with the life of Mary Magdalene, and remain among the most potent symbols surrounding her image today. Alabastron, the famed "alabaster jar" of the scriptures, has become the signature trademark of Mary Magdalene through the centuries. Christian painters often show her with an alabaster jar or spice box, and she is often featured with a small vessel called a chrism, a jar or vessel that holds special aromatic spices and perfumed ointments.

Certain anointing oils and perfumed ointments, such as spikenard and myrrh, are often neglected in theological writings and discussions about Mary Magdalene. Yet they lie at the heart of the image of her that has come down to us from biblical times. Such perfumed oils and ointments are also central to Christianity, in that the very act of the anointing of Jesus was the acknowledgment of his messianic status, as the New Testament states. Several famous biblical scenes describe an anointing of Jesus by an unnamed woman with an alabaster jar, with one of them naming this woman as Mary of Bethany, the sister of Martha and the resurrected Lazarus. Anointing customs were part of a very ancient tradition. Spikenard and myrrh feature prominently among the various perfumes and oils listed in the Song of Songs, for example. Anointing the dead was a traditional part of Judaism and such rituals also featured in many ancient Eastern cultures.

The ritual anointing of Jesus by a woman with precious spikenard ointment is referred to in the Bible and was clearly understood by the disciples to be an especially significant ritual act, yet, at the time, they expressed strong resentment about the use of such a highly expensive perfume oil for this anointing. Jesus defends this woman on every occasion, reminding them

Jesus defends the anointing woman, in the face of the Apostles' clearly expressed strong resentment of her extravagance.

that this anointing by her not only foreshadowed his impending death in a messianic context—obviously a key event in his entire ministry—and, he also told them, as the accounts in Mark and Matthew relate, that wherever the Good News is proclaimed, what she has done will be told 'in remembrance of her." Jesus was commenting on the importance of what she had done in spite of any human imperfections that she might have had. But he also felt it was a loving and devoted acknowledgement of his mission, and reminded the disciples that what she had done would be told in remembrance of her. Therefore, not only was this ritual anointing act of great importance to his mission, in that it was a foreshadowing of his death, but it was also the very act for which this woman herself would be remembered in the future.

The Anointing Woman

There is still much debate about whether the biblical scenes of a woman anointing Jesus were in fact referring specifically to Mary Magdalene. But no one—from any side of the theological debate—has ever disputed that the anointing(s) of Jesus were very important events, if not central to the overall messianic mission of Jesus. Despite this, we may never know the precise identity of the woman who anointed Jesus, as she is unnamed in three of the four biblical passages.

In the fourth scripture passage (John 12:1–8), this woman is referred to as Mary of Bethany, about whose identity there is also much debate in the Western Church, specifically regarding whether or not she is the same woman as Mary Magdalene. Mary Magdalene is not specifically named in connection with an anointing until after the Crucifixion, at the tomb on Easter morning. In the past, many theologians believed that it was certainly plausible that Mary of Bethany may have been the same woman as Mary Magdalene.

▼ A nineteenth-century engraving of Jesus with Mary of Bethany.

There are several important references to an anointing scene of Jesus by a woman in the synoptic Gospels—Matthew (26:6–13), Mark (14:3–9), Luke (7:36–50)—and in John (12: 1–8). Although we may never know the identity of the anointing woman with the alabaster jar, in every single one of these biblical episodes she brings precious oils, ointments, and pungent spices as a crucial component of the ritual anointing ceremony that is central to Jesus' ministry.

For many centuries the Eastern Orthodox Church has maintained that the three anointing women of the scriptures were entirely separate individuals. Even today, it still has different

◀ The myrrophores, each carrying an alabaster jar, arrive outside the tomb on Easter morning.

feast days for each them, with St. Mary Magdalene's feast day on the same day as that devoted to her in the Western Church, 22nd July. Protestant Churches generally reject all of these specific definitions or are far more indifferent. So in several of the key biblical anointing scenes the rather mysterious anointing woman is either unnamed, or she is called Mary of Bethany. But in the best known scriptural accounts about Easter, especially Mark 16:1, Mary Magdalene is specifically named, in particular in reference to her bringing myrrh and precious spices on Easter morning. Such acts of anointing were central to the life of Jesus and his mission—"Christ," from the Greek *Christos*, and the Hebrew word *messiah*, both mean "Anointed One."

The alabaster jar and its contents

In ancient times certain precious oils or expensive perfumed ointments were often kept in jars or boxes made of alabaster stone. Major museums house examples of these types of vessel from many cultures of the ancient world. As the perfumed ointments and oils were very expensive luxury items—often more valuable than gold—the alabaster jar would have been very carefully sealed; particularly if it was to be used in a ritual anointing context, as it was in the New Testament. So there is an additional factor in the anointing scenes of the Gospels that should not be overlooked—it was the breaking open of this alabaster jar and its seal at the anointing of Jesus that also made it a highly significant act. The anointer had to be very careful as to when and under what circumstances she would

► During the first century perfume was often stored in stone or glass vessels. These alabasterons would have held about a pound of ointment.

open such a vessel. The disciples were also aware of this fact, as obviously this woman had brought her unopened alabaster jar of the most costly, precious oil available, for the precise purpose of breaking it open specifically for the ritual act of the anointing of Jesus, signifying that this was a most special occasion.

The significance of spikenard

Such precious oil or ointment of spikenard would have been saved for very important guests and also for a very special purpose. According to museum curators, in many cases, once the seal had been broken, the entire alabaster jar would automatically break into many pieces, spilling out all of its precious contents. This would usually occur only if the anointer had deliberately chosen to spill all of the contents. It is specifically commented on in the scriptures that the entire room was fragrant with the lovely spikenard perfume—this would have

▲ Jesus disputes the significance of his anointing with the disciples as the anointing woman dries his feet with her hair, her empty jar clearly visible by her side.

been because the whole vessel had been broken open, spilling out a far larger quantity of precious perfume than the few ritual drops that would normally have been used.

We know from the New Testament accounts that the disciples objected to what they felt was an extravagant waste of such precious oil—but again, the use of this oil would have been the whole point from the anointer's perspective, since the ritual anointer had to save this jar and its precious contents exclusively for this, and only this, very special occasion. She would have believed that only the very best would do to anoint the Lord. For this woman to have sacrificed an extremely expensive jar and its entire precious contents was, in the context of the time and with regard to Jesus himself, her way of expressing that only the very best was suitable for him for this special ritual anointing occasion. But the disciples did not immediately grasp the overall significance of this in the same way that Jesus did, and were astounded at the apparent extravagance of the woman, commenting that the oil could certainly have been sold for the benefit of the poor. Yet, in spite of his disciples' criticisms, Jesus defends this woman's actions in every instance.

Now one of the Pharisees asked Jesus to have dinner with him, so he went into the Pharisee's house and took his place at the table.

Then when a woman of that town, who was a sinner, learned that Jesus was dining at the Pharisee's house, she brought an alabaster jar of perfumed oil. As she stood behind him at his feet, weeping, she began to wet his feet with her tears. She wiped them with her hair, kissed them, and anointed them with the perfumed oil.

Now when the Pharisee who had invited him saw this, he said to himself, "If this man were a prophet, he would know who and

◄ Mary Magdalene anoints Jesus' feet in this detail from Alessandro Bonvicino's (1498–1554) *Banquet at the House of Simon.*

▶ Jewish burial rites include the anointing of the body before it is wrapped in a sheet and buried.

what kind of woman this is who is touching him, that she is a sinner." So Jesus answered him, "Simon, I have something to say to you." He replied, "Say it, Teacher."

"A certain creditor had two debtors; one owed him five hundred silver coins, and the other fifty. When they could not pay, he canceled the debts of both. Now which of them will love him more?" Simon answered, "I suppose the one who had the bigger debt canceled." Jesus said to him, "You have judged rightly."
Luke 7: 36–43

Certain jars and boxes were also used in the context of burial rites, but in the New Testament, the alabaster jar used by the anointing woman is referred to only in relation to messianic anointing and not in connection with burial rites.

Perfumes and oils have long been used in many religious ceremonies the world over to demarcate the "before" and "after" moment of an important ritual time or event. Even today, a special perfume ritual called *Havdalah* is an important symbolic closing ritual of the Sabbath, signifying a time of very clear differentiation between the holy time of the Sabbath and the other secular days of the week. So the special anointing of Jesus with spikenard was one such moment in his ministry and involved the use of perfumed ointment and an alabaster jar or box.

The enduring image of Mary Magdalene with her alabaster jar is truly symbolic of the significance of anointing rituals in biblical times. But it wasn't only the jar that was important. The precious contents of the jar—spikenard and myrrh—have been associated with Mary Magdalene throughout the ages.

▶ The burial of Christ is depicted in this seventeenth-century Russian embroidered silk panel entitled *The Entombment.*

▼ A havdalah set, used in the ritual for the closing of the Jewish sabbath.

Spikenard and Myrrh

One rarely hears much about perfumes and spices in theological or religious discussions and writings about Mary Magdalene, even though spikenard and its renowned qualities for healing and calming would seem to perfectly fit the purpose and mission surrounding the anointing of Jesus. For this obviously most important mission—the anointing of Jesus—the mysterious unnamed woman with the alabaster jar carefully, and very specifically, chose spikenard, to symbolize the extraordinary and challenging messianic mission ahead of him, and ultimately involving, of course, foreknowledge and awareness of his death.

Spikenard

**O my beloved, you are like a mare
among Pharaoh's stallions.
Your cheeks are beautiful with ornaments;
your neck is lovely with strings of jewels.
We will make for you gold ornaments
studded with silver.**

**While the king was at his banqueting table,
my nard gave forth its fragrance.**

Song of Songs 1:9–12

Spikenard is mentioned in the Song of Songs, the New Testament, and other ancient writings. A costly perfume used for the anointing of Jesus, it was a prime choice among the fine precious oils that had long been in use for anointing, healing the sick, or embalming the dead in many ancient

◀ Mary Magdalene with her alabaster jar, a depiction by Flemish painter Rogier van der Weyden.

▼ A relief carving of medical herbalists at work. Traditionally, they would have provided healing oils, such as myrrh.

Mary Magdalene was a woman of means, as indicated by her elaborate hairstyle and ermine collar and cuffs in this stylized painting by Francesco Bacchiacca (1494–1557).

cultures. Spikenard, or "nard" as it is also referred to today, is a perennial plant that comes mainly from India; in biblical times it was brought in alabaster boxes to the Holy Land from the Himalayas, a great distance from Palestine. As it was very expensive, it was used only by the wealthy at the time of Jesus. Many theologians now believe that Mary Magdalene was one of the wealthy women of means who supported Jesus' ministry, so she and her circle would certainly have been able to afford luxury items like spikenard.

Spikenard has long been used in many cultures as a healing plant; it is known as *nalada* in Sanskrit, *nerd* in Hebrew, *nardin* in Syriac, *nardos* in Greek, and *sunbul hindi* in Arabic. The Hebrews and Romans were also known to have used it in certain burial rituals, although in accounts of the use of spices, perfumes, and oils for burial rites in the ancient world, myrrh features much more prominently. Spikenard oil was produced through a special distillation process from the rhizomes of a rare plant with purplish-yellow flowers, *Nardostachys jatamansi*. As a large quantity of this rare Himalayan plant was required for the extraction of a very small amount of oil, it was very expensive to produce, especially in biblical times, and then it had to be shipped all the way back to Palestine. By the time of Pliny's famous Natural History (A.D. 70)—a botanical source, well known in the Middle Ages, that discusses thousands of plants, including spikenard—direct Roman trade with India had increased greatly, helping to bring down the price. Roman perfumers used spikenard, too, in their famed oil of the ancient world, *nardinum*.

In a number of ancient cultures, spikenard was associated with both marriage and burial rites in addition to playing a key role in certain holy anointing occasions. So it is perhaps not all that surprising that the special anointing of Jesus was performed specifically with calming, healing spikenard oil.

◄ Wealthy ancient Romans, both male and female, spent enthusiastically and extravagantly on perfumes and cosmetics.

Myrrh

Myrrh features in the earliest known Magdalene wall painting, dated approximately A.D. 240, and entitled *Myrrophore*. This image was not discovered until 1929; it was found at Dura–Europos on the river Euphrates in Syria, and was moved a few years later to the Yale University Art Gallery at New Haven, Connecticut, where it can still be seen today.

▼ Many cultures used myrrh and frankincense in their rites and rituals. Here, incense is being used in a traditional Jewish ceremony.

Myrrh, a bitter-tasting resin, is derived from the Hebrew word *murr* or *maror*, meaning bitter. Its genus species is *Commiphora myrrha* and its family is *Buseraceae*. Originally believed to have come from Punt, encompassing areas now known as Ethiopia, Eritrea, or Somalia, much of it may also have been sourced in southern Arabia, Oman, or Yemen. Frankincense and myrrh came mainly from Arabia. Many would come from far and wide to buy myrrh and other valuable spices and incenses from Arabian merchants. The powerful and wealthy Sabeans of ancient Mesopotamia, renowned for their knowledge in a variety of areas, may have been a key part of this trade as well—Jacob of Edessa (d. A.D. 708) specifically identifies Saba as the homeland of myrrh, frankincense, and other spices.

As it is a resin—also referred to as an aromatic gum—myrrh does not decay. When it is burned it creates an aromatic smoke. In ancient times, it was highly valued as a ritual incense and perfume, and was as valuable as gold, if not more so. Myrrh was one of the gifts brought by the Three Wise Men (Magi) to the infant Jesus.

Myrrh features, together with spikenard, in many famous verses of the Song of Songs, for example 4: 12–15:

Your branches are an orchard
of pomegranate trees heavy with fruit,
flowering henna, and spikenard,
and saffron, cane, and cinnamon,
with every tree of frankincense,
myrrh and aloes, all the rare spices.

▲ The Magi present their gifts to the newborn Christ child in this fourteenth-century panel by Italian painter Bartolo di Fredi.

Easter morning

Myrrh has long associations with embalming and funerary rites in many ancient traditions, and it is specifically mentioned in all of the accounts that Mary Magdalene and the myrrhophores brought myrrh to the tomb on Easter morning to finish their final anointing rituals. It was probably the major spice brought there by the women.

The first use of myrrh occurred at the entombment of Jesus' body, just after the Crucifixion, when Nicodemus is described as bringing aloes and myrrh (John 19:39), which were wrapped up with the

▼ Jesus is anointed with myrrh and aloes prior to being wrapped in linen and entombed. The distress of the women is evident in this work by Peter Paul Rubens.

linen, which was then wrapped around Jesus' body. This was the entombment process, and after this procedure had been finished, the body was laid to rest. The spices were not only for embalming, however, as according to Jewish law, bodies must return to the earth, so anything that acts to prevent or retard decomposition is avoided in the embalming process. The spices are believed to have been used in embalming procedures primarily to offset the scent of death that would have been a problem in such a warm climate. Bodies were ritually cleansed and entombed, usually in a rock-hewn tomb, where they were left for about a year, after which the family would take the bones and place them in an ossuary.

Corpses were considered unclean under Jewish law, so it fell to the kinswomen of the deceased to prepare bodies for burial. In Jesus' case the anointing process that was started on the evening after the Crucifixion had probably been hurried, perhaps even curtailed, in observance of the Sabbath law requiring Jews to be in their homes by sundown on Friday. At dawn on Sunday morning, according to the scriptures, three women returned to the tomb where they had left

▲ Spices were used by the ancient Egyptians in their elaborate embalming procedures. Here, the jackal-headed god, Anubis, who is particularly associated with mummification, embalms a body.

▶ Mary Magdalene, carrying her alabaster jar of spices, arrives at the empty tomb, which is guarded by an angel. The crucifixion site can be seen in the background.

the body, bringing their myrrh and special spices, fully prepared, despite the turmoil and despair into which the followers of Jesus had been plunged after the Crucifixion, to finish the final ritual anointing of his body for burial. And, as we know, they were astonished to find nothing but an empty tomb.

These three loving and dutiful women—Mary Magdalene, Mary the mother of James, and Mary Salome—are specifically named in Mark 16:1 and John 20:1–18. Mary Magdalene was the very first person to encounter the risen Christ and she then proclaimed the news of the Resurrection to the disciples (Mark 16:9–11).

▲ A stone carving on a pillar in the basilica at Vézelay, which shows Mary Magdalene being tempted by the devil (left) and being saved by a monk.

Now on the first day of the week, at early dawn, the women went to the tomb, taking the aromatic spices they had prepared. They found that the stone had been rolled away from the tomb, but when they went in, they did not find the body of the Lord Jesus. While they were perplexed about this, suddenly two men stood beside them in dazzling attire. The women were terribly frightened and bowed their faces to the ground, but the men said to them, "Why do you look for the living among the dead? He is not here, but has been raised! Remember how he told you, while he was still in Galilee, that the Son of Man must be delivered into the hands of sinful men, and be crucified, and on the third day rise again." Then the women remembered his words, and when they returned from the tomb they told all these things to the eleven and to all the rest. Now it was Mary Magdalene, Joanna, Mary the mother of James, and the other women with them who told these things to the apostles.

Luke 24:1–11

◄ This engraving by Gustave Doré depicts the three Marys descending to the tomb and finding the angel outside.

Epilogue

DISCREDITED AND REVERED IN TURN BY THE CHRISTIAN CHURCHES, MARY MAGDALENE CONTINUES TO FASCINATE US TODAY AS HER STORY CONTINUOUSLY UNFOLDS.

The Magdalene mythos in the making—then and now

Like a crystal with many facets, the changing faces of Mary Magdalene and her powerful legacy have left us with the most powerful mythos of the sacred Feminine ever witnessed. And the time of her greatest popularity of all in the West—the High Middle Ages—has given us a variety of perspectives. For many reasons, it was precisely in that period that the cult of St. Mary Magdalene really grew and developed. Yet it was also then that she first became a focus of mass adulation, often being a key attraction of the colorful medieval Easter guild plays. By the time of the Renaissance, she was still a favorite subject for paintings, depicted with her trademark alabaster jar at her side.

Far from being a "Dark Age," the High Middle Ages, while admittedly feudal in structure and the time of the Inquisition, was also a time of culturing flowering in other areas. It was the time when the great cathedrals were built; the era of the Knights Templar, of Richard the Lionheart and the wars of the Crusades, the writing of the Arthurian Grail romances, the end of the Cathars,

▼ The three Marys arrive at the entrance to the empty sepulcher, and are told by the angels that Jesus is risen.

◀ Mary Magdalene is often
depicted with a skull, recalling the
Crucifixion, which took place at
Golgotha, the Place of the Skull.

▶ A thirteenth-century French manuscript, the bottom half of which shows Mary Magdalene preaching to the Apostles.

the Troubadours, the writing of the Zohar. Like Mary Magdalene, the High Middle Ages has also often been seen in a derogatory way, misunderstood or disparaged, unfairly maligned at times, or viewed through a narrow lens. Yet, in fact, it too had many facets and many coexisting events and movements, and the rise and prominence of Mary Magdalene was one of these.

Among the most popular medieval shrines of all were those of St. Mary Magdalene. Occasionally, virtual stampedes would occur at her shrines. Tales and traditions of many healings, conversions, and miracles of the power of St. Mary Magdalene have come down to us from this time, promoted as they often were by kings and influential noble families. We encounter her in pageants, miracle plays, and fairs; we find major basilicas and private chapels named after her; we hear of pilgrims' shrines and unique Magdalene traditions; we see her prominence in stained-glass windows and carvings in major cathedrals; we come across her relics in both the East and the West; we learn of the Black Madonna shrines, her own special pilgrimage sites, medieval guild symbolism, and examples of how her continuing legacy of power and beauty endured well into the Renaissance, when she was a key feature in many famous paintings.

▲ The Black Madonna of Rocamadour, a French pilgrimage site in the Lot region. The sculpture dates from the late twelfth century.

The process continues today, as her mythos continues to develop, change, and adapt. Far more recent times have brought other more fascinating and controversial, if not historically documented, views of

171

Mary Magdalene to the fore. Yet, as many will attest, she still beckons people today, calling us to whatever facet of her story we are drawn to. Like many saints' lives, her story has been created over many centuries, a combination of different scriptures, tales, and legends. It has fascinated, lured, and challenged. In our own modern, secular age, as we clearly witness the rising popularity and greatly increasing interest in all facets of Mary Magdalene, her universal mythos might in

▼ Mary Magdalene arrives in France, a detail from the sixteenth-century altarpiece of *Saint Magdalen*, now housed in the Cathedral Museum in Girona, Spain.

fact be a bit closer to the Woman Who Knows the All—from the earthly and sensual, to the highest divine. With Mary Magdalene, many point out today, nothing is excluded or sanitized. She has the full range of feelings, characteristics, and attributes to which modern individuals can relate. She is seen as a realistic guide to spiritual development, as an inspiration to increased consciousness of God, meditation, and prayer, and even, at times, to conversion to Christianity today.

Mary Magdalene's special care for those on the margins, the exiled, the black sheep, and the downtrodden has long been commented upon by pilgrims. Perhaps it is not all that surprising that in certain areas, shrines and pilgrimage sites that are relevant both to St. Mary Magdalene and to the Black Madonna traditions are located near each other.

▲ A pensive image of the saint, painted by Italian artist Carlo Dolci (1616–1686).

The steadfast faith, loyalty, truth, and wisdom of Mary Magdalene are for everyone, devout or secular, male or female, young or old, of one faith or none. A Christian saint as well as a key metaphorical embodiment of the return of the biblical Sophia Wisdom, Mary Magdalene still inspires and challenges today. Her enduring faith, truth, and light are forever unfolding, as her universal mythos continues to evolve in the twenty-first century.

Reference

WIRFF DEN ERSTEN STHEIN AVF SIE · IO VIII

Glossary

Act of Peter A short miracle story, celebrating virginity, found in the fifth-century Codex of Berlin. It relates a legend, said to be about the crippled daughter of Peter; however, many scholars today believe that this particular text has little or no relation to the Peter of the New Testament.

Alabaster jar A special small vessel used by women in Middle Eastern and Mediterranean regions in late antiquity and biblical times to carry perfumes, oils, or unguents, often used in funerary rites. The jar is also referred to as an "alabastron." In Christian art, the vessel often shown with Mary Magdalene is called a "chrism."

Apocryphal texts Texts believed to fall outside of the officially recognized canon. A collection of apocryphal books is often known as "Apocrypha." Just as there are different religious traditions there is no one Apocrypha— in Christianity the Apocrypha refers to texts that were included in the Greek Old Testament but not in the Hebrew Bible; the Catholic Bible includes the apocryphal books but calls them "deuterocanonica," and the Protestant Bibles generally exclude all of the apocryphal texts. New methods of textual analysis and more recent discoveries show that some books labeled "apocryphal" in earlier periods of Christianity are as or more authentic than some that made it into the canon.

Apostola apostolorum Translated as "apostle to the apostles," a term denoting the key role of Mary Magdalene in telling others about the Risen Christ. She was the first person to witness the risen Christ and was told by him to inform the other disciples about the Resurrection.

Bernard of Clairvaux An influential French medieval Cistercian abbot and doctor of the Church. He was born at Fontaines-les-Dijon in 1090 and died at Clairvaux in 1153. Arguably one of the most extraordinary Western Christian Church leaders and orators, Bernard was also a very strict monastic ascetic, often railing against excesses of wealth or character. Tireless in his dedicated spiritual work and extensive writings as well as his more famous worldly activities, he spearheaded the founding of over

70 Cistercian monasteries. He was the major advocate to the Pope for the fledgling Order of Knights Templar, and he assisted them with writing their early Rule. He is especially remembered for his famous controversy and stimulating arguments with Abelard, a leading proponent of a more scholastic and rational approach to spirituality. He was commissioned by the pope to preach the Second Crusade. Canonized in 1174, Bernard is recognized as a saint and venerated by Roman Catholics and Anglicans on his feast day, August 20th.

Bethany The village that has been described as the home of siblings Mary, Martha, and Lazarus.

Canon A list of officially sanctioned authoritative books accepted as Holy Scripture by the Church—for Roman Catholics, this was determined at the Council of Trent in 1546; although there is no official Protestant canon, some individual denominations have determined their own list(s).

Cathars Gnostic heretics of the twelfth and thirteenth centuries who challenged existing medieval Church doctrine more than any other contemporary movement. Particularly strong in southern France and northern Italy, with various groups throughout Latin Christendom, the Cathars held the dualist belief that the earthly, physical world was evil, and that humans are therefore "trapped" in a material prison of the body. Release from this condition occurred through the ceremony of the *consolamentum*, which allowed one to return to one's guardian spirits in Heaven. They included women in their priesthood of "parfaits," and had a powerful healing tradition, a vegetarian diet, and an ascetic lifestyle. They had a fervent belief that the existing Church was corrupt, evil, and power-hungry and this placed them at odds with the Church and led to their persecution and a major Inquisition against them, which began in earnest in the thirteenth century, and culminated in the burning alive of many Cathars at Monségur in 1244.

Desposyni A term used to refer to the alleged family of Jesus, descended from King David, including his cousin John the Baptist and his brothers as named in the New Testament, James the Just, Simon, and Jude.

Dialogue of the Savior Believed by many scholars to date from the second century, the sole existing copy of this badly damaged manuscript describes a dialogue between the Savior and the circle of some of his closest disciples, including Judas, Mary, and Matthew. It was discovered near **Nag Hammadi** in Egypt in 1945.

Feast Day of St Mary Magdalene Celebrated each year on July 22nd in the Western and Eastern Christian churches; however, in their myriad traditions, the Eastern Orthodox church also celebrates the translation of the relics of St. Mary Magdalene on May 4th.

Gospel There are many gospels, both canonical and non-canonical; the New Testament synoptic (meaning "with the same eye") Gospels are Matthew, Mark, and Luke.

Gospel of Mary The sole existing example of an early Christian text written in the name of a woman—Mary—now believed by most, but not all scholars, to be Mary Magdalene. A German translation first appeared in 1955, and an edition in English was finally published in 1977, as part of the **Nag Hammadi** texts. This Gnostic work emphasizes the teachings of Jesus as a path to inner, mystical knowledge, and also portrays Mary Magdalene as a visionary and capable leader within the circle of Jesus' disciples. This text addresses challenging topics surrounding issues of Church authority and leadership, including the role of women in the Church, a contentious issue in many religious traditions even today.

Gospel of Philip Found near Nag Hammadi in 1945, the Gospel of Philip features a great variety of topics, including specific teachings of and about Jesus, early Christian baptism, parables, bridal chamber ritual, etc. This work also makes reference to Jesus and Mary Magdalene in a far closer context than most others. Harvard theologian Professor Karen King and other textual experts today maintain that the overall theological views of this manuscript largely fit with those of the disciples of Valentinus, thus dating the work to the late second or early third century.

Gnosis Gnosis is a Greek word meaning "knowledge" or "wisdom," especially of a directly inspired, intuitive nature rather than one resulting from a purely intellectual approach that focuses on external doctrine or analysis. In general, it might be better understood today as a profound inner experience, and/or as a continuing process of personal "revelation," whereby one seeks union with God or the Infinite, and to know the reality behind the Reality. In the early centuries of Christianity, there were many different groups that identified themselves as "gnostic." Gnostics usually placed a high premium on individual experience and revelation and had a greater appreciation of the feminine, leading to serious clashes with orthodoxy.

Gnostic Gospels A modern term for the important texts found in Egypt at Nag Hammadi in 1945. Although many ancient Christian texts have long been identified as "gnostic" in nature and have been criticized, studied, burned, or esteemed for centuries, today they are considered to be early non-canonical texts or apocryphal texts about the life of Jesus, and thus remain as controversial as they are fascinating. Some of the key Gnostic Gospels, highlighting Mary Magdalene in particular, include the **Gospel of Mary** and the **Gospel of Philip**.

Kabbalah The mystical aspect of Judaism, central to which is the Tree of Life; the **Zohar** is generally regarded its most important text.

Knights Hospitaler A religious order founded in Jerusalem in 1099, especially devoted to medical care for pilgrims and to fighting in the battles of the Crusades. Together with other Christian knights they defended the Holy Land from the Saracens, and, after its fall in 1291, went first to Cyprus and then on to Rhodes. In 1523, they were given the island of Malta by Emperor Charles V but were driven from there by Napoleon in 1798. Today they are more popularly known as the Order of St. John and still focus on emergency medical care and other activities; their headquarters is in Rome, with various branches worldwide.

Knights Templar The Order of the Temple (1119–1312) was a medieval military religious order that existed during the time of the Crusades. Arguably the largest, wealthiest, and most powerful organization outside of the Church in the Western world at the time, its members were dedicated monastic warriors, bankers to kings, trusted diplomats, farmers, transporters and protectors of pilgrims, business scions, navigators, and more. At its height, their empire consisted of over two thousand commandaries in Europe alone, with more in the Holy Land. Popular and greatly respected for their many victories in battle, inevitably their immense wealth and power became the envy of many, including the French king, Louis X. In 1307, the leading knights were arrested and accused of many crimes, initially only in France, and then in other countries as well. After several years of brutal imprisonment, torture, and a series of lurid trials of its members, the Order was finally suppressed on foot of a papal bull in 1312, although the Pope's final verdict was that the charges against the Templars were "not proven."

Madeleines Said to have been Marcel Proust's favorite snack, these light, shell-shaped cookies are made in honor of Mary Magdalene, in a special "madeleine pan." Food has long had religious, spiritual, and folkloric significance, with certain recipes specifically made in honor of the saints. See also **navettes**.

Magdala The often disputed location of the town where Mary Magdalene and her family may have originated; however, scholars maintain that there is no definite connection between the saint's name and a place called "Magdala."

Manicheans A dualistic sect that followed the teachings of Mani (A.D. 216–277). St Augustine (354–430) was a Manichean before he converted to Christianity.

Meretrix A term meaning "prostitute" and not the term used for Mary Magdalene by Pope Gregory in his sermon of 591, which was *peccatrix*, meaning "a sinful woman." Nowhere in the New Testament does it state that Mary Magdalene was ever a prostitute.

Merovingians Arguably the most powerful and the longest-lasting early medieval Frankish kingdom (481–751), the Merovingians have nonetheless received little recognition in Western history, largely owing to the hostility of the Church as well as that of the Carolingians who usurped them. They were known to be strongly Arianist (nontrinitarian) in their beliefs, and were thus in disagreement with the traditional Nicene Creed.

Mercator The medieval term for a seller of medicinal cures and cosmetics, also known as an apothecary.

Myrrophores Literally, "bearers of myrrh," the dedicated and devoted women who brought myrrh and other special spices to the tomb of Jesus to conduct their burial rituals.

Mythos A belief system or cluster of archetypes that forms over time around a specific idea, person, or organization, a kind of "mystical aura," which develops a life of its own. It often incorporates elements of both historical fact and legend; many would argue that there is still a strong mythos around the concept of the medieval order of the **Knights Templar**, or around especially powerful or charismatic individuals in history or literature such as King Arthur, King Solomon, and, in more recent times, Mahatma Gandhi.

Nag Hammadi An Egyptian town near where, in 1945, important ancient parchments were found by a local farmer in sealed jars in a cave. The Nag Hammadi Library (see also **Gnostic Gospels**) is a collection of 13 ancient codices (books), which includes 52 texts.

Navettes Since 1781, at Les Four des Navettes near the Abbey of St. Victor in Marseilles, small boat-shaped pastries known as navettes have been made, in honor of Lazarus, Martha, and the two Marys. Each year, on February 2nd, the archbishop of Marseilles blesses an oven full of these pastries, and, according to tradition, the Black Virgin appears ten days later in the chapel at St. Victor's.

Pistis Sophia A manuscript that describes a major visionary post-Resurrection dialogue between the Savior and a circle that included his closest disciples, in which Mary Magdalene features prominently. Many scholars maintain that it was probably composed in the third century, and was included in the fourth-century parchment book known as the Askew Codex, discovered in the eighteenth century.

Priory of Sion Historically an obscure traditional Catholic chivalric order founded during the French Fourth Republic, but more commonly associated with a mystical secret society whose aim was to restore the Merovingian dynasty to the thrones of Europe and Jerusalem, an idea popularized in books such as *The Holy Blood and the Holy Grail.*

Sepulcher An archaic term for a tomb or burial place.

Shekhinah In Judaism, the indwelling presence of God, very often described as the feminine aspect of the Godhead. The Shekhinah also has a special role in **Kabbalah** studies and the Tree of Life. Similar Christian concepts are the Holy Spirit, or aspects of the Greek Sophia.

Shrines In the medieval period, Christian pilgrims were strongly encouraged by the Church to visit shrines of major saints. A box or special container for housing a relic or sacred artifact, a shrine is also a special, enclosed area in a church, cathedral, or temple, often a reliquary, dedicated to a particular saint. Shrines were often located in major Gothic cathedrals or in churches on the road to Santiago de Compostela or Rome, and medieval pilgrims often visited a number of sites.

Skull In Christian iconography of Mary Magdalene, a skull (together with a book and a bell) is often portrayed alongside the saint. Many art historians believe that as Golgotha—Place of the Skull—is also clearly connected to the Crucifixion of Jesus, the imagery of the skull was associated with Mary Magdalene.

Sophia From a Greek word meaning "Wisdom," Sophia has long been an important concept in the writings of both orthodox and unorthodox Christianity, Greek philosophy, Gnosticism, and in the works of Plato. Sophia is seen as an integral aspect of the holy Trinity (the Father, Son, and the Holy Spirit); others, especially from Greek Orthodox tradition, hold that Sophia is the same concept as the Logos, Christ. As the mystical feminine aspect of the Godhead, Sophia is also perceived by some Christians as the Bride of Christ, as, for example, in the writings of the medieval Rhineland abbess and mystic, Hildegard of Bingen. In the West today, there is a revival of interest in the entire Sophia concept as well as in the divine feminine aspect of God. In kabbalistic writings, *hokhmah* (wisdom) often appears along with the term *shekhinah*, the (feminine) indwelling Glory of God, and bears a strong similarity to the Christian concept of Sophia.

Troubadours A class of medieval lyric poets who flourished principally in France from the eleventh to the thirteenth centuries. They composed poems and songs in the "langue d'oc," chiefly on themes of courtly love.

Wisdom of Solomon The collection of wise sayings long attributed to King Solomon of biblical times, yet written in Greek in the first century A.D.

Zohar An important kabbalistic text in the Spanish Toledo Tradition, believed by many scholars to have been written in medieval Aramaic in the late thirteenth century by Moses de Leon. Widely acknowledged as a profound work of great insight and mystical perception, "zohar" is from a Hebrew word meaning "splendor and radiance," and is a series of mystical texts commenting on the Torah, the five books of Moses.

▶ Mary Magdalene was present when Jesus was taken down from the cross. In this *Deposition* by Raphael she can be seen on the Saviour's left side.

Bibliography

Aquinas, St. Thomas, *Summa Theologiae*, vol. 55, London: 1976 ed. C. Thomas Moore O.P.

Angold, M., *Byzantium: The Bridge from Antiquity to the Middle Ages*, London: Phoenix Press, 2001

Armstrong, K., *A History of God*, New York: Mandarin, 1993

Atwood, R., *Mary Magdalene in the New Testament Gospels and Early Tradition*, Bern: Lang, 1993

Augustine, St., *The City of God*, London: Penguin, 1986, trans. H Bettenson

Baker, D. ed., *Medieval Women*, Oxford: Oxford University Press, 1978

Barber, M., "Origins of the Order of the Temple", *Studia Monastica* 12 (Barcelona, 1970)

_____, *The Cathars: Dualist Heretics in Languedoc in the High Middle Ages,* Harlow: Pearson Education Ltd, 2000

_____, *The New Knighthood: A History of the Order of the Temple,* Cambridge: Cambridge University Press, 1994

Begg, E., *The Cult of the Black Virgin*, London: Penguin, 1985, rev. ed. 1996

Begg, E. and D., *In Search of the Holy Grail and the Precious Blood,* London: HarperCollins, 1995

Bellevie, L., *The Complete Guide to Mary Magdalene,* New York: Alpha Penguin, 2005

Bennett, C., *In Search of Jesus,* London and New York: Continuum, 2001

Bennett, R. F., *The Early Dominicans: Studies in Thirteenth-Century Dominican History,* Cambridge: Cambridge University Press, 1937

Birnbaum, L. C., *Black Madonnas: Feminism, religion and politics in Italy,* Lincoln, N. E.: ToExcel publishers, 2000,

Boyer, M.-F., *The Cult of the Virgin,* London: Thames & Hudson, 2000

Carr-Gomm, S., *The Dictionary of Symbols in Western Art,* New York: Facts on File, 1995

Chilton, B., *Mary Magdalene,* New York: Doubleday, 2005

De Boer, E. A., *The Gospels of Mary,* New York: Harper San Francisco, 2006

Forey, A., *The Military Orders from the Twelfth to the Fourteenth Centuries,* Basingstoke: Macmillan, 1992

Freke, T., *Wisdom of the Pagan Philosophers,* London: Journey Editions, 1998

Jansen, K. L., *The Making of the Magdalene: Preaching and Popular Devotion in the Later Middle Ages,* Princeton: Princeton University Press, 2000

King, K., *The Gospel of Mary of Magdala: Jesus and the First Woman Apostle,* Santa Rosa, CA: Polebridge Press, 2003

_____, *What is Gnosticism?,* Cambridge, MA: Harvard University Press, 2003

Kraemer, R., and D'Angelo, M. R., eds., *Women and Christian Origins,* New York and Oxford: Oxford University Press, 1999

Lambert, M., *The Cathars,* Oxford: Blackwell, 1998

Le Loup, J.-Y., *The Gospel of Philip,* Rochester, VT: Inner Traditions, 2004

_____, *The Gospel of Mary Magdalene,* Rochester, VT: Inner Traditions, 2002

Langland, W., *Piers the Ploughman,* London: 1966, transl. J. F. Goodridge

Markale, J., *Cathedral of the Black Madonna,* Rochester, VT: Inner Traditions, 2004

Mango, C., ed., *The Oxford History of Byzantium,* Oxford: Oxford University Press, 2002

Manniche, L., *Sacred Luxuries: Fragrance, Aromatherapy, and Cosmetics in Ancient Egypt,* Ithaca, NY: Cornell University Press, 1999

Marjanen, A., *The Woman Jesus Loved: Mary Magdalene in the Nag Hammadi Library and Related Documents,* Nag Hammadi and Manichaean Studies XL, Leiden: E. J. Brill, 1996

Mead, G.R.S., *Pistis Sophia,* Mineola, NY: Dover Publications 2005

Merkur, D., *Gnosis: An Esoteric Tradition of Mystical Visions and Unions,* New York: University of New York Press, 1993

Meyer, M., *The Gospels of Mary: The Secret Tradition of Mary Magdalene, the Companion of Jesus,* San Francisco: HarperSanFrancisco, 2004

Milburn, R., *Early Christian Art and Architecture,* Berkeley and Los Angeles: University of California Press, 1988

Moreira, I., *Dreams, Visions and Spiritual authority in Merovingian Gaul,* New York: Cornell University Press, 2000

Mouilleron, V. R., *Vézelay: The Great Romanesque Church,* New York: Harry Abrams, Inc., 1999

Miller, M., *Chartres Cathedral,* Norwich: Jarrold Publishing, rev. ed. 2002

Nicholson, H., *The Knights Hospitaller,* Woodbridge: Boydell Press, 2001

Nilson, B., *Cathedral Shrines of Medieval England,* London: Boydell, 1998

Pagels, E., *Adam, Eve and the Serpent,* London: 1988

_____, *Beyond Belief: The Secret Gospel of Thomas,* New York: Random House, 2003

_____, *The Gnostic Gospels,* London: Penguin, 1985

Palmer, A., *St Mary Magdalen Oxford: A Thousand years of a church and parish,* Oxford: St Mary Magdalen Restoration and Development Trust, 2001

Potter, D., *Prophets and Emperors: Human and Divine Authority from Augustus to Theodosius,* Cambridge, MA: Harvard University Press, 1994

Ralls, K., *The Knights Templar Encyclopedia,* New Jersey: Career Press 2007

Ricci, C., *Mary Magdalen and Many Others: Women Who Followed Jesus,* Minneapolis: Fortress Press, 1994

Rouse, R. H. and M. A., *Manuscripts and their Makers, Commercial Book Producers in Medieval Paris* 1200–1500, London, 1999

Selwood, D., *Knights of the Cloister: Templars and Hospitallers in Central-Southern Occitania c.1100––1300.* Woodbridge: Boydell Press, 1999

Schaberg, J., *The Resurrection of Mary Magdalene: Legends, Apocrypha and the Christian Testament,* New York and London: Continuum, 2002

Shlain, L., *The Alphabet versus the Goddess: The Conflict between Word and Image,* New York: Viking Penguin, 1998

Schmidt, C., *Pistis Sophia,* Nag Hammadi Studies 9, Leiden: E.J. Brill, 1978

Schwartz, L. C., *The Fresco Decoration of the Magdalen Chapel in the Basilica of St Francis of Assisi,* PhD diss., University of Indiana, 1980

Spencer, B., *Pilgrim Souvenirs and Popular Badges,* London: Museum of London, 1998

Spufford, P, *Power and Profit: The Medieval Merchant in Europe,* London: Thames & Hudson, 2002

Starbird, M., *The Woman with the Alabaster Jar,* Rochester, VT: Inner Traditions, 1993

_____, *Mary Magdalene: Bride in Exile,* Rochester, VT: Bear & Co., 2005

Steffler, A.W., *Symbols of the Christian Faith,* Grand Rapids: Wm. B. Eerdmans Publishing Co., 2002

Stoyanov, Y., *The Other God: Dualist Religions from Antiquity to the Cathar Heresy,* New Haven, CT: Yale University Press 2000

Thiede, C. P., and D'Ancona, M., *The Quest for the True Cross,* London: 2000

Thompson, M. R., *Mary of Magdala,* New York: Paulist Press, 1995

Torjesen, K. J., *When Women were Priests Women's Leadership in the Early Church And the Scandal of their Subordination and the rise of Christianity,* San Francisco: Harper and Row, 1993

Van der Broek, R., and Hanegraaff, W. J., *Gnosis and Hermeticism: From*

Antiquity To Modern Times, Albany: State University of New York Press, 1998

Verdon, J., *Travel in the Middle Ages,* Notre Dame: University of Notre Dame Press, 2003, trans. Geo. Holoch

Voragine, de Jacobus, *The Golden Legend: Readings on the Saints,* Vols I and II, Princeton: Princeton University Press, 1993, transl. Wm. G. Ryan

Wakefield, W. L., and Evans, A. P., *Heresies of the High Middle Ages,* New York: Columbia University Press, 1969

White, E, *The York Mystery Plays,* Yorkshire Architectural and York Archaeological Society, York: Ebor Press, 1991

Wink, W., *Cracking the Gnostic Code: The Powers in Gnosticism,* Society of Biblical Literature Monograph Series 46, Atlanta: Scholars Press, 1993

Index